DYNAMICS OF DEVELOPMENT

DYNAMICS OF DEVELOPMENT
A Sociological Perspective

S.R. Mehta

GYAN PUBLISHING HOUSE
NEW DELHI - 110002

Dynamics of Development - A Sociological Perspectives

(*Sociology, Management*)

ISBN : 81-212-0681-0

Published in 1999 in India by
Gyan Publishing House
5, Ansari Road
New Delhi – 110 002

Laser Type Setting at : Sita Fine Arts Pvt. Ltd., Delhi – 110 052

Printed at : Chawla Offset Printers

CONTENTS

PREFACE

As a sociologist, I have travelled a long journey in the realm of development. Nearly half of this journey was in action sociology while the other half had been in the academic sociology. In fact, I learnt my lessons of sociology from my nearly two decades of field work in development processes related to agriculture, health, population and rural development. These practical experiences provided me rich insights into human aspects of development. While, later in the academic of sociology, I started realizing that sociology is short in theory and long in praxis.

No doubt, the theory and the method of any discipline go together but in respect of sociology, my experience is that the theory in sociology is inadequate, has weak explanatory power and is mainly guided by the predilections of the scholars pursuing it, whereas the methods of sociology have contributed significantly in understanding the complexities of human relationships. Perhaps, the roots of sociology are strongly embedded in its methodology to generate empirical facts and attempt at building a theory is only a part of the exercise on the sociology of knowledge.

It is observed that over theorization often makes an otherwise good empirical study and there is a need to provide a judicious mix of theory and empirical data generated through appropriate sociological or anthropological methods.

The essays in this book have been written during my academic journey in sociology. My interest in relating theory to practice is in the manner of reverse swing. In other words, those theoretical formulations which could suitably explain the sociological issues in the field situation have been highlighted. Moreover, these may be more amenable than others to the practitioners of sociology in the development of human groups.

The present work, therefore, presents a happy blending of theory and practice in analysing issues related to dynamics of development. As these essays have been written over a period of time, there may be repetition of some ideas and thoughts but at times, that is necessary to strongly reinforce certain issues and perspectives.

Many of the essays in this book have been published earlier. It is hoped that in the larger interest of community of scholars, the publishers of these will allow me to reproduce them here in anticipation of their nice gesture, I am grateful to them for the same. I am also thankful to Professor R.M. Sethi, Chairperson, Department of Sociology, Panjab University for extending support to me in this work. I also take this opportunity to thank my wife, Saroj and daughter Rani, in supporting me in this venture.

S.R. Mehta

1

Sociology of Development

The Concept of Development: The Emerging Concerns

Development is a slippery concept. Although, much of the writings on the subject flowed down the academic stream, yet the concept remained elusive. By and large, the difficulty lies in it being conceived differently by scholars belonging to different disciplines. One is constrained to operationalize it for empirical validation as with time and space, the concept goes on acquiring complexities in its nature and forms. However, it has its connotations in biology and economics. In both of these dimensions, it is an evolving concept. In its physical sense, it emphasizes differentiation in shape and form, moving from simple to complex structural forms and on the factor of heredity for suitable adaptation of Man to his environment.

The need for survival is the uppermost in Man's mind and in order to eke out his existence on this plane, Man has to deploy his physical and mental energies to exploit the environment in which he is placed, to his advantage. This economic activity on his part, apart from other basic needs like food, sex and shelter, brings human beings together and sets in the process of group formation. The group formation, in due course of time, gets institutionalized through normative patterns which regulate the behaviour of groups to realize the commonly arrived goals operationalized in terms of needs of its members. The plethora of human needs goes on multiplying and the Men endeavour to utilize all resources at their disposal command (Men, Money and Material) to accomplish the needs of their respective groups.

With the transformation of Men into knowledgeable and skilful persons, they evolve technology, moving from primitive to modern forms, and acquiring almost a near command over their respective environments on the earth. This sets in the process of development of Man, and that of his environment. In his interaction with his environment, Man through the active involvement of actors, agents, agencies and institutions usher in the structurization process of a society for the perpetuation of its enlarged population in an ever expanding and articulating economic and socio-cultural activities through controls , or influences of political structures or substructures, built up in the process.

At this juncture, the philosophical question often posed is whether transforming Men will lead to societal development or alternations in the societal arrangements would throw up individuals and create new institutional structures for the development of society. Both these orientations have given rise to different schools of thought in sociology and most of these perspectives (I would prefer to call these perspectives rather *than* theories as in strict scientific sense, it is difficult to visualize a theory in Sociology) veer around either of these orientations. However, these orientations, theories, constructs and meta theories are often influenced by the predilection of scholars, their training and background. Of late, there has been attempts made by scholars to view social formation processes while analysing the social conditions in which human beings are placed for interaction in different settings, situations and contexts and build up structures of human interactions by taking into account the societal as well as the personal factors, thereby suggesting a convergence between the socio-centric forms and an individual's orientations, motivations, and goals. The dilemmas and contradictions thrown up by these two sets of perspectives in Sociology for analysing and understanding human society, often, have posed difficulties in building up socio-cultural aspects of development of a society.

Society is complex, unpredictable because of a large number of uncertainties observed in the role structures of actors, agencies and institutions and often is influenced by situational contingencies which remain, by and large, unexplained due to variations observed in them in social space and time. Moreover, our society is basically a moral society and being so is always circumscribed by the regimens of conformity and non-conformity, in conceiving more developed from the less developed on the normative plane.

In economic parlance, development is conceived in terms of growth of economic goods and services necessary for a good society characterized by more of pleasure and less of pain to its people and a conducive atmosphere for leading a harmonious life. However, there are ideological underpinnings even amongst the economists belonging to capitalist and socialist paths of development. Though both aim in providing a good society, yet their methods or approaches to development of societies are different. Marx, in his economic analyses, suggested transformation of societies from feudal through capitalism to socialism and communism. But this type of analysis is not acceptable to the modern economists who tend to rely heavily on hard economic indicators for assessing the development of nations.

Growth strategies were evolved which emphasized on rapid industrialization and consequent urbanization, commercialization of agriculture through generation of surplus food items, international trade, technological innovations, markets for capital, labour, goods and services and above all, the entrepreneurial development among the motivated persons to produce more for national consumption and beyond for export to other nations in need of such a produce. The growth of wealth, goods and services were measured in terms of Gross National Product (GNP), per capita income or other national accounting figures. The God of GNP, dominated the development scenario of the western nations and it was suggested that the growth strategies adopted by these nations will equally develop the developing nations.

However, despite increase in GNP of these nations, they could not tackle the problems of unemployment, malnourishment, poverty, illiteracy and income disparities in their respective nations. Instead, these nations embraced all the vices and ills of the western developed nations and many of the methods or strategies of development in these nations resulted in maldevelopment or they proved anti-developmental. The growth strategies of the developed world assumed that by a rise in GNP, the socio-cultural and political configurations will be taken care of automatically, as was experienced in the developed world but in the context of the developing nations, these assumptions proved wrong.

Historical circumstances leading to long colonization of most of these nations, rigid social stratificational realities and social structural and organizational arrangements, vested interests of the elite class, traditional centres of power structures and values embedded into the religious ethos and cultural themes of these nations posed counter productive movements and processes to the growth strategies, as these nations were largely agricultural-based communities with strong social networks and cultural traditions. As for the such, they were not a amenable to the economic growth model of development. Growth may be a necessary condition for the development of a nation but it is not a sufficient one. Apart from raising the GNP, one has also to take into account the socio-cultural and political configurations that these newly developing nations have thrown up after independence from the colonial rules to which they were subjected for centuries.

However, the independence of these developing nations brought in the political governance as a frontrunner factor for development inasmuch as the economic interests became subservient to the political interests. The power élities in these nations followed a policy of adhocism and inorder to keep themselves in power positions, they were guided by factors other than the development of their respective nations. To keep the vote bank with them (as most of these nations followed democratic pattern of governance), they called upon the economists to plan such programmes and projects that suited their political designs rather than the felt needs of the people. Economists played a second fiddle to the political masters of these nations and in this sense, the value system and the social organizational arrangements of people in these nations, were also ignored.

This raises an important issue, whether we can conceive of development in a universalistic sense or we have to treat it as culture specific. The concept of cultural relativism and the sense of ethnocentrism attached to each of the cultural group, that the cultural anthropologists have provided us, make us better aware and knowledgeable about the ways of living of people across cultures and within cultures. Notwithstanding, many differences and similarities within and across nations, each society has to conceive of development in its cultural framework and in consonance with its value system. Any attempt at the development of a society not in congruence with the culture of its people, is likely to be thrown out. As such, cultural imperatives, as causes and consequences of development, need to be taken up seriously along with improving the material conditions of people. This will also include the moral and the non-material dimensions of culture as well.

Moral implies developing values among people to distinguish between right and wrong on the basis of norms evolved within a society, develop ethics of conforming to the right and instil in people the elements of courage, discipline and confidence to do the right rather than a wrong. The moral standards have to be set by each society and it is this dimension that makes development a value-based concept. It is a difficult task to lay down the moral standards of a society. Economic tastes of the people may be assessed in terms of needs of existence and other associated hierarchical or horizontal needs of people. However, the most daunting task is to find out the social preferences of the people. These are value loaded and what is right for one group, may be wrong for another group. Apart from that, there are shifting emphasis from one type of value to another and in a given social space, over a time period, there may be changes in the values prevailing in different societies.

Cross-cultural studies through indepth and longitudinal research designs are necessary for assessing the changes in the values of the people. Studies of such a nature are scanty and make development a difficult proposition within the cultural perspective. Besides, values are dynamic and not static and the element of dynamism throws up contradictions of various kinds which need to be resolved through institutionalization of new structures for an integrated social living. Social life based on value consensus rather than on dissensions should be promoted for a new social order. This does not mean, that there is no role of dissensions for a social life. In fact, the dissensions should lead to newer development of values based on consensus. A new social order based on material and moral dimensions and through transformation of Men and Societies, should be what development must aim it, otherwise it will remain maldevelopment for any society.

An exhaustive social commentary on the conceptualization of development should lead us to examine the different theoretical constructs on it, thrown up by scholars to capture various instrumentalities and expressiveness associated with its formulation and operationalization.

While reconsidering the concept of development, it is argued that "development" is a historical phenomenon born at a specific moment of history in a specific economic and cultural framework. The concept was generated by the social and economic mind-set formed during the process of worldwide "internationalization." However, there is a need to consider development and its opposite "underdevelopment" in the context of the Third World nations and instead of transferring the western values in a wholesale manner onto them, there is a need to the blossoming of the indigenous cultures of these nations (Batubenga, 1993). This is development specific to culture of different nations. The underlying argument is that instead of treating development in terms of material dimensions, it should be viewed as what people of a particular culture can contribute to humanity at large.

The first two development decades based on economic: growth and modernization "paradigm" showed some promising outcomes for the developing nations. However, in the late sixties and early seventies of this century, serious doubts were being cast on the development rationale as reflected by the Club of Rome's Limits to Growth Report and Robert McNamera's (Ex-President, The World Bank) admission that despite an increase in GNP in many of the developing nations, the poorest segments of the population had the least benefit out of it. This became evident from the startling revelation that the developing countries by mid 1980s were forty-five times poorer than the industrialized ones. It was suggested that the four decades of development strategies have not brought any fundamental changes in the lives of the poor, particularly so in Africa.

There is, now a hue and cry, for the validity of the concept of development. Scholars have started questioning the very legitimacy and rationale of development and it is argued that there is a need to enter into ethical debate on development and thrash out basic questions about equity, social justice and probity, so crucial for the developing nations for their progress or advancement (Carmen, 1994).

Improvement in the quality of life of people through developing some of the welfare indicators like life expectancy at birth, infant mortality, birth and death rates, enrollment of boys and girls in schools, literacy levels especially among women, and levels of nutritional standards to diminish malnourishment especially among mothers and children, also formed a part of the development strategy, without taking into account the structural and cultural impediments embedded in the social structure of these nations. This formed part of the basic human need approach for the development of people of these nations.

Food, shelter, health care, education and participation of people in development initiatives were suggested as a part of integrated development. But, due to historical circumstances especially the long impact of colonialism in terms of extraction of wealth and creation of collective inferiority in these nations, the ecological, cultural and social structural contradictions contained in the western industrial conception of development, were sidetracked. Economic development fostered a creation of elite class in these nations . The elites further contributed towards the impoverishment of people by exploiting, oppressing and discriminating them to enjoy the entire benefits of development initiatives only for themselves. The radicals, among the development thinkers, suggested dimensions such as equity, social justice and probity as key elements in the concept of development. But, there are practical difficulties in accomplishing these because of inherent inequalities built into social systems of the nations, vested interests of the persons in the power positions and other social and cultural considerations. There is a need to deconstruct the power relations embedded in the idea of development and make development free of its social Darwinian view of the past and future. Instead, the thrust should be to mobilize the contribution of traditional raw materials of development in a society such as labour, women, children and the environment (Inayatullah, 1994). This will make development a participatory concept.

While treating environment as a resource, one is increasingly convinced that with rapid industrialization and urbanization, there is an imminent threat to the natural environment of the developing countries. Growth strategies have promoted consumerism and this has led to exhaustion of natural resources. In short, the growth strategies, liberalization and market economic forces have impinged heavily on human ecology and there is an immediate need to bridge economics and ecology with the social life of these nations. The attempt to establish linkages among these three—ecology, economic and social life—is what is called 'Sustainable Development' (Mehta, 1997). In essence, it means, development of the present generation of people in these nations, without affecting the future generations.

Poverty, unemployment, illiteracy, malnourishment and threat to natural environment are the basic problems of the developing nations. As such, any conception of development will become meaningless till all the impossibilities and possibilities about them are tackled on a well-informed basis within the cultural framework of a society. As such, development, as a cultural process should be conceived in terms of including elements such as natural environment, social relations, production, consumption and distribution, education and social well being of people.

Development of a nation has to be environment friendly. Overexploitation and overexhaustion of the natural environmental resources can play havoc with the development of the people as depletion of resources on this finite planet will have dangerous implications for the future generations. Besides, to improve the quality of life of people, infrastructural development such as construction of dams, canals, power, energy, roads, telecommunication, airways, waterways, irrigation networks, etc., is significant but this may lead to involuntary displacement of population causing in them landlessness, joblessness, homelessness, marginalization, increased morbidity, food insecurity, loss of access to common property and social disarticulation (Cernea, 1997).

Besides, development being environment friendly among human beings, social relations are fundamental for the existence and perpetuation of a society. Group cohesiveness, social solidarity, harmony, cooperation are necessary prerequisites of an integrated social living. But that does not rule out conflicts, tensions and dissensions in social life. However, these need to be resolved and accommodated through a negotiated set of understandings among people to build up confidence, trust and integration. Social arrangements are also necessary for the production process. Growth strategy is essential for the development of a society as without capital formation, development may remain a far cry. However, the production of goods and services should be in consistence with the needs of the people as in societies, where needs give rise to demands, false modernization effects become visible (Mehta, 1981).

The resultant effect will be increased income disparities, concentration of wealth in a few hands and large segment of the population getting impoverished. This can only be corrected if the equitable distribution of goods and services could be made possible in the developing nations. Economic theory has a stronger explanatory power to analyse the production and consumption behaviour of people. However, it is weak so far as its explanation of distribution of goods is concerned. The theory needs to be reexamined in order to take care of equity, social justice and probity for these segments of population who are poor, underprivileged, exploited and discriminated on the basis of age and gender. Social equity also warrants gender equity as almost half of the population in the developing nations constitute females. The problems of poverty and unemployment can be tackled by increased participation of labour force in the production of goods and services and in equitable distribution of the same in different groups.

Education is a critical factor in development. Education not only promotes cultural heritage from one generation to another and performs a historical function, but it also helps in building personality structure of individuals as well as it provides them up the with an identity to have a better expansion of and control over their resources.

Illiteracy is hampering the development. Technical knowledge and skills, besides general awareness, can go a longway in the increased production processes. Besides, better educated people are more conscious of the problems faced by the population they are associated with and this provides them an edge over others to place their needs in a meaningful manner before the policy planners and administrators. In this regard, gender equity in education is most desirable as an educated mother can always be an asset in building up a nation. Moreover, educated persons can show better commitment than others in development initiatives and these factors can promote participatory process through people's organizations in the development of these nations.

Apart from catering to the some of the other social well-being of certain specialized groups such as women, youth, landless labourers, handicapped and mentally retarded persons, and socially underprivileged, disprivileged and discriminated persons, there is a strong need to take care of the health care of the people. A healthy nation is a productive nation. Health care, especially of expectant mothers, infants, toddlers and children, if handled with care and dynamism, can be instrumental in solving the problem of malnourishment among the developing countries. This is highly correlated with the problem of poverty and illiteracy in these nations. Last but not least, the social well being of people can be taken care of only if we provide a check on the population growth in the developing nations. Population growth infringes adversely both on the poverty and the environment of these nations. If population growth surpasses the economic growth of a nation, it will act as a menace and the ghost of Malthus will prove disastrous for it.

In short, the construct of "development" should include environmental, economic and non-economic parameters in its delineation. Thus environment, social relations, economic growth with distributive justice, education, health care and population control become the basic elements essential for conceptualising development in the context of developing nations. Non-economic parameters such as social, structural and organizational arrangements and value system of the people in a given society through human resource development, process of education and other welfare measures such as health care and population control, are essential elements in promoting economic growth with distributive justice. Thus, the emerging scenario justifies the conception of development as economic are seized with the limitations of their growth theories and are convinced of the significance of socio-cultural factors in the development process. They have realized that without a change in the socio-cultural systems of these nations, economic growth may not be a possibility. As such, development for these nations will have to be cultural specific and in consistence with local values, aspirations and efforts of the people. However, the multi-dimensionality of the concept poses difficulties in its operationalization for empirically measuring it in specific cultural groups.

Sociology of Development: Theoretical Formulations

After the delineation of the concept of development, one may like to examine the theoretical concepts related to the sociology of development.

Sociology, as a discipline, has evolved to analyse and understand the patterns of actions and interactions between human beings. For any action to take place, there are certain prerequisites to be met. First, there is need for the physical or social setting where the action may be initiated by an individual. Secondly, there is a need for a plurality of actors, minimum two, to set on the action process. Effective communication between the actors and regulated through norms, values and standards evolved by the group or the society, make the interactions directed towards predetermined ends or goals mutually decided by the members. This leads to the establishment of social relations.

These, over a period of time and within a social space, become relatively stable, institutionalized into organizational arrangements for the fulfilment of societal needs. The relative invariance in social relationships observed in regulative or operative institutions are thus abstracted to delineate the social structure of the society. The interrelatedness of institutional elements within the societal structure when there is interdependence in between different parts to represent the whole, constitute a social system. As there is an interdependence of parts to the whole, each social system has a structure and a function to perform. The structure in the social system is represented by the "status" and the function by the "role" that the actors occupy and are required to play respectively, to throw up a configurations of social relationships and establishment of institutional networks.

This structural-functional perspective was in vogue with the early sociologists and anthropologists. They, through field observations, and using analytical categories studied various social phenomena and their relatedness to understand the social ways of life. Based on empirical findings, they were able to abstract certain generalizations regarding the social structure of groups, village communities and tribes. These synchronic studies, subsequently, examined by diachronic studies, showed certain continuities and changes in the way of life of people. As such, continuity in and changes of social structure of societies, became the twofold dimensions of sociological investigations. While studying various social phenomena in the community or the society, depending upon the unit of analysis, they have made attempts to analyse the factors that go in the causation of a particular social phenomenon or a series of phenomena and the consequences that phenomenon or series of phenomena have on the social life of the people. However, the sociologist has to do the construction of that social phenomenon within his theoretical or analytical framework and operationalize it empirically to validate it.

Sociology as a discipline has a Euro-American tradition. The theoretical formulations have been influenced by enlightenment thinkers, philosophical foundations, epistemological methods, and hermeneutics. The earlier sociological analysis on "Development" was influenced by the Euro-American traditions in sociology. However, the problems of development of the Third World nations, especially of the Latin America, attracted the attention of some scholars to provide an alternative perspective on the Sociology of Development.

The theoretical formulations on Sociology of Development, are a post World War Second phenomenon since it is only after that the concept of development got currency. Earlier, the level of living index was being employed to differentiate the development levels of the nations. Notwithstanding the limitation of the sociological theories which are inadequate to capture the total social reality due to lack of objectivity, and difficulties in experimentation, verification and validation of social concepts for a generalization on society as close to the scientific investigations of physical or biological sciences, yet appropriations to scientific concepts and methods are made by combining a number of social theories (Grand, Middle Range and Empirical based) to explain the processes of continuity and change in a society as there is not a single theory coherent in nature that could explain the social phenomenon of social change. As such, it may be safer to talk of perspectives in sociology rather than theories in sociology as advocated by some of the purists in the discipline.

The great economic depression of 1929-30 was tackled with Keynesian macroeconomics while the post World War II development phase was mainly guided by the "Modernization" paradigm largely influenced by the concept of economic development. It was believed that this may help eradicate poverty from the planet. Some of the main clichés associated with this paradigm, have been rapid industrialization, urbanization, modernization, big push and take off into self-sustained growth. This continued till 1970s when it was realized that the globe is facing a megacrisis due to unlimited economic growth on one side and that of social and ecological collapse on the other. Efforts were made to bridge the gaps between economics, ecology and social life and this brought in the concept of sustainable development (Maxneef, 1990).

The thrust on 'sociology of development' has been to examine the persistent economic and social inequalities between the developed and the developing countries. Different perspectives have been thrown up by sociologists to reduce these inequalities, recognize their permanence and speak for their functionality in the operation and growth of the global economy. It is suggested that the present evolution of global economy and slight concern over natural development is in correspondence with some of the sociological theories of the past. The first generation sociologists especially of the North America related progress during 1950 to the process of modernization. Development was considered to instil the "right" orientations—values and norms, in the non-western societies so as to enable people in these countries to partake in the modern wealth-creating economic and political institutions of the advanced West

(Portes, 1977).

No doubt, this early sociological perspective did show promise in predicting the diffusion of modern western orientations and institutional forms to the less developed world. But on certain fronts, 'Modernization' theories did not predict in the right direction because it was observed that instead of sustained economic growth and greater social equalities, the modernization process for these developing nations resulted in indicating several unexpected negative consequences such as the rising levels of consumerism among the population not in consistence with their productivity levels, bifurcation between elites able to participate in modern consumption and masses aware of but excluded from it and increased migratory processes as individuals and families were pulled towards centre of modernity of the developed countries (Portes and Walton, 1981, Roberts, 1978).

There is no one 'Modernization' theory. In fact, the term refers to a variety of perspectives that were applied by non-Marxists to the Third World in the 1950s and 1960s. Evolutionism (with its focus on social differentiation), diffusionism, structural functionalism, system theory, and interactionism all combined to help develop the mish-mash of ideas to be known as the 'Modernization' theory (Harrison, 1989).

In the modernization theory, there are three main streams, one advocated by economists, the other projected by sociologists and the third supported by the social-psychologists. Among the economic modernists, the prominent were Hoselitz, Gunnar Myrdal and Rostow. Hoselitz, apart from highlighting, the interrelationship between economic and cultural change in influencing effects of western technology on non-industrial societies, also supported Parsons analysis, that the economic roles in the underdeveloped countries are particularistic, functionally diffused, ascriptive and self-oriented. Unless these roles of the actors in these countries are changed to that of the actors in the western societies, the economic growth may not occur (Hoselitz, 1960). However, the impediments to the development with developing nations, are their internal social structural and cultural factors. Hoselitz, ignored the factor of colonialism, and the overriding economic and political structures within which the underdevelopment of these countries is situated (Frank, 1969).

Myrdal, treated, the Asian developing countries as soft states and vouched for institutional and attitudinal changes of people in these societies (Myrdal, 1970). Rostow (1960) gave five stages through which all societies have to go through to attain economic growth of the level of western-industrial nations. In the first stage, in most of the developing countries, output is limited due to the lack of access to science and technology, values are generally fatalistic and political power is non-centralized while the second stage is a "pre-take off" one where new ideas promote progress through education, entrepreneurship and institutions necessary to mobilize capital investments especially in transport, communication and raw material, leading to commercial expansion. The third stage is a "take off" stage where traditional barriers to economic growth are overcome through new technology and emergence of new political groups committed to the modernization of the economy. While the fourth stage refers to "The Drive to Maturity" which is indicative of nearly 10 to 20 of national income invested in development and the economy taking over the international trade. The last stage is that of high consumption, specialization in manufacturing of durable consumer goods and services. His theory has also been criticized because of ignoring the historical and structural factors of the underdeveloped countries (Frank, 1969).

Among the sociologists, the concept of Calvinism given as a part of Protestant Ethic giving rise to capitalism, is one of the significant contributions that Weber could make to the progress of the western industrial nations (Weber, 1930).

Parsons's contribution to evolutionary universals as prerequisites of the existence of any human society are well-known. According to him, for a human society to exist at all, there should be a necessity for certain basic and universal requirements of any human being. These are: religion, a particular language for communication, social organization through kinship and technology (Parsons, 1964). However, Parsons considers technology in its most undifferentiated form.

To him, technology is nothing but synthesis of empirical knowledge and practical techniques and these represent the culture of the society. In short, the humanity has the ability to create and transmit its culture. Later on, as a society becomes more complex, and gets urbanized, social stratification and new forms of legitimization, are the added evolutionary universals. With further evolution of societies, there is greater specialization in areas such as bureaucratic organisation and the emergence of money and the money market and the democratic associations. These may increase further the adaptive capacity of the societies and move them away from primitiveness and provide a lead to a universalistic order depicting modernity. However, in the context of developing nations, one cannot expect bureaucratic organizations and democratic associations to be free from ascriptive bonds (Harrison, 1989).

Another sociologist, Neil Smelser, a student of Parsons, advocates structural differentiation, social integration mechanisms and social disturbances as the major processes of social change and modernization as the developing countries more towards rapid industrialization. However, to check the inevitable social and political instability as a result of modernization of such societies, he rallies around a strong centralized government which should promote the value of nationalism and expect the masses to sacrifice and resist from making protests (Smelser, 1965). This sounds somewhat not pragmatic in the prevailing situations.

Lerner's stress as "empathy" as a factor of modernization is well known. For him, one of the essential aspects of modernization is the development of mobile personality characterized by rationality and empathy. Mass media act as a "mobility multiplier" and is supported by factors such as high degree of literacy, urbanism, media participation to increase "empathy" of people to move towards modernization (Lerner, 1958). The factor of "creativity" by Hagen (1962) "achievement motivation" by McClelland (1961), Inkles "Modernity syndrome" characterized by new experience, openness, innovation, democratic attitude, an orientation to future and to things other than that of immediate relevance, planning one's life, a determination and belief to dominate environment and achievement of goals, control over the world because it is calculable, belief in the dignity of other especially women and children, belief in scientific knowledge and temper and a belief in distributive justice, are well documented and stressed upon (Inkles and Smith, 1974).

A greater role in these theories, has been on treating individuals as change agents or on the role of modernising elites as prime movers of modernization, innovation and its diffusion and on industrialization as a process of social change while the focus on analysis in the context of developing nations has been on social and cultural impediments to change. The overemphasis on endogenous rather than exageneous factors of change and the neglect of structural historical circumstances belied the expectations associated with the paradigm of "Modernization" to reduce social and economic inequalities embedded in the social structure of the nations.

It is the second generation of sociologists, not belonging to the North American School but from the Latin America who reacted sharply to the predictive errors of the "Modernization" paradigm. These scholars were heavily influenced by the Marxist political economy framework. Modernization by these scholars was viewed as an extension of western capitalist ideology and its impact on the rest of the world especially the developing countries, kept them in the permanent state of backwardness. Underdevelopment of the developing nations was viewed as a consequent of the development of the developed nations as these nations actively managed the modern industrialization process in such a manner as to keep the terms of trade primarily in their favour and to the detriment of primary producers of goods in the weaker nations. The sociology of underdevelopment, as it is called, was propagated by Marxist economists such as Frank (1978), Baran (1973), Amin (1976).

These dependency theorists (as the developing nations were considered dependent on the economies of the developed nations) set aside all considerations of values and ideas and held responsible the economic interventions of the multinational corporations and their parent governments, for the poverty of the Third World nations. This see-saw theory, popularly known as dependency theory, no doubt, correctly predicted the increasing global hegemony of MNCs and international capitalist institutions. The peripheral countries of Asia, Africa and Latin America, by and large, remained dependent on the external capital flows of the core developed countries and on the economic directions of the international financial organizations; yet this theory failed to account for the promotion of autonomous industrialization of these nations and the successful experience of some of the "most dependent" Asian countries. In the first instance, the import-substitution models of development in these countries to counteract external capitalist penetration, through state intervention, did not show results while in the second case, the 'Asian tigers', through skilful reinscription got in the global trade, exploited the comparative advantages of the trade in their favour (Portes, 1997). The failure of import-institution model is attributed to jumping of the protectionist tariff barriers by the multinational corporations to compete directly with the local firms. However, it is difficult to explain the experiences of the "Asian tigers" that promoted successful industrialization drive by opening themselves to global trade and vigorously driving low-cost industrial exports. However, the latest experiences of these "Asian tigers" barring Japan and Singapore in mismanagement of financial resources, non-accountability and non-transparency in financial matters, due to nepotism and favouratism of the elites, has put the economy of some of these countries in shambles.

It is argued that of the existing sociological analysis, the world-system theory has been more closer than any other in predicting the general trend of events during the last quarter of century. Wallerstein (1979) and his followers, always argued that the real unit of analysis has to be the capitalist world economy that had its roots within the European state system of the sixteenth century, encompassing the entire globe. This evolved global system created nations including those of the Third World, and determined their development positions in the international hierarchy. As such, it makes no sense in speaking of national development of these nations as the only entity that "develops" is the capitalist world economy (Wallerstein, 1979).

The world-system model assigned little weight to population factor in these nations as sheer number is likely to affect the relative power of States. Instead, the thrust has been on trade flows among nations, their relative geographical advantages, and their military and technological strength. However, as predicted by this theory, during the last half a century or so, there has been acceleration of flows of information, technology, trade and labour on a universal scale binding populations of disparate regions together. Also, Wallerstein contention that socialism, as it unfolded in the erstwhile Soviet Union, was not a counter system at all; rather it represented a bold but a failed strategy to gain ascendance in the global capitalist system. This can explain the collapse of the socialist states of Eastern Europe (Portes, 1997).

The tendency of the developing countries, in the present set up, to insert themselves in the global financial markets to avoid economic and political marginalization, appears to be in relevance with the world-system approach. This perspective, in contrast to dependency theory which advocated partial withdrawal from the world economy to have autonomous industrialization within the import-substitution policy, has an edge over other sociological perspectives to analyse the contemporary development scenario. However, its resolute focus on long-term historical evolution and the postulate of a single unit of analysis, appear to be the main limitations.

Most of the problems, dilemmas and decisions of the development take place at the intermediate level of the nations and communities trying to cope up with their particular situations. To place the sociological study of development properly in the context of present realities, there is a need to abandon modernization versus dependency debates and go beyond sweeping statements. Instead, a greater attention should be given to factors of domestic order, including characteristics of nation-states, the relationship of states with classes in the civil society, population size and density (Portes, 1997). This type of analysis will bring us closer to conceiving development within a national milieu, springing up from the nation's own heart, and nurturing on its own resources of Men, money, material and means.

Another group of theorists now hold that for genuine and authentic development, there is a need for an ethno-development strategy based on grassroot socio-political movements and popular culture. Such an ideology is due to the efforts of some strongly committed social action groups. Here, the communication is mainly of interpersonal type and occurs in a group rather than at the mass level. Such a communication sensitizes people and encourages their participation and decision-making in development initiatives for an affirmative action (Mehta, 1992).

Currently, the development theorists are seized with a model of communication policy that should foster political, economic and socio-cultural negotiation and integration. This perspective visualizes the formation of a common national culture as a basis for national development. Further, the role of mass media is viewed as a kind of public cultural ritual, for negotiating cultural conflicts and agreeing on common values (Servaes, 1986; White, 1990).

Notwithstanding the theoretical relevance of the sociology of development, for the development of the Third World countries, one must recognise the fact that none of these are mutually exclusive and they do influence the thinking process of the scholars predilected to one school of thought or the other.

On the basis of analysis made of the Sociology of Modernization and Development, some emerging themes on the subject are suggested. First, there is a constant tension between individual actors and the social systems which they form part of. Although people make their own history and they are purposeful actors, yet their actions do not produce results of their own choosing. Secondly, the continuing process of industrialization, whether in a capitalist or in a socialist state, is a clear indication of modernization and occupies a central place in all perspectives on development. Thirdly, the culture of the people cannot be ignored. What people learn in their social setting about production and government and nature of their beliefs, values and social moves cannot be treated as a 'superstructure' relying on economic 'base'. What people eat, drink and choose to purchase, sell or exchange is a matter of economic necessity. In short, economic behaviour has always to be situated in a cultural context. Fourthly, it is worthwhile that a sociological perspective on development should focus both on objective (social, economic and cultural contexts in which individuals operate) and subjective (focussing actors in development) aspects. Fifthly, there is a need to revive the linkages in the concepts of diffusion, and innovation. Cultural diffusion across developed and developing nations as a two-way process should not be underrated in a development perspective. Finally, sociologists should return to the political structures and the political leadership (Harrison, 1989). Not only the role of elites but that of emerging rural leadership, relating development to the need structure of people, is a desirable focus (Mehta, 1972).

Sociology of Development: People's Agenda and Action

The sociology of underdevelopment or the under-development theory, advocated either by the dependency theory or its sister variant world-system approach, has been criticized both by the Marxist as well as by the non-Marxist scholars. The concept of capitalism is the major bone of contention between the underdevelopment theorists especially that of world-system approach and the Marxist scholars. Marxist argue that the relations of production within the capitalist system have been ignored both by Wallerstein and Frank, and the capitalism has been confused by them with the existence of an economic system. Further, the factor of unequal exchange is secondary in the development and maintenance of capitalism which rests on the productivity of its free labour force. No significance has been given to this fact. In this context, the Marxists scholars are critical of the world system theorists of treating class formation and class struggle as residual categories in their analysis. The focus on national and international contexts of class struggle has been neglected and a return call has been made by Marxists to treat the nation-State as a unit of analysis rather than the global capital list system. This brings us back to class conflict existing within the indigenous social structures of the developing nations, for development purposes. Even, at the empirical level, there are some Marxists who argue that the underdevelopment theory is inadequate in its interpretation of the empirical data on the Third World development. In fact, the development is taking place and capitalism is fulfilling its historical mission. The problem of development in them is not because of their dependency on the developed world but due to internal contradictions of the Third World within itself. In short, the Marxists are critical of the world systems theorists who, unlike, them, studied relations of the 'core' with the 'periphery' while they concentrated on the capitalist 'core' countries, to the neglect of the socio-economic structures of the Third World and misinterpretation of the nature of capitalism (Harrison, 1989).

The non-Marxist criticism of the world systems approach is manifold. First, it is argued that basically, this theory is tautological in the sense that if formal colonialism was responsible for the underdevelopment of the Third World, then one can illustrate the point that countries that had avoided colonial domination, were more 'developed' than the other parts of the Third World. But the world system's theory rules out any kind of such a division because of the belief that capitalism has peneterated every Third World nation irrespective of the presence or absence of colonial background and the nations have been categorized as colonies, semi-colonies or neo-colonies. Even the nations of Eastern Europe and China have been incorporated into the world system. Secondly, the relationship of dependency of the developing nations on the developed nations has nothing special to offer as every society, to a certain extent is, dependent on others. Rather, the relationship in between all nations, irrespective of development or underdevelopment is that of interdependence. Thirdly, the non-economic linkages of the 'periphery' to the 'centre' cannot be ignored and these will be contingent upon the specific cultural characteristics of the developing nations. Unfortunately, the world system theorists have considered all social action and interaction and culture to representing some kind of objective economic interest and this appears to be non-convincing. Finally, like Marxists, the non-Marxists also feel that empirically speaking, development can and does take place in the Third World and it is directly linked with the formation of close ties with the 'core' societies. It is argued that as and when these ties are broken or become weak, the underdevelopment of the periphery nations increases. Moreover, there is failure of the dependency theory to deal adequately with the transfer of technology and the role of values and diffusion in development . These arguments take us back to the position which the modernization theory occupied

(Harrison, 1989).

A succinct review of the critiques provided on the sociology of underdevelopment (dependency theory or world systems theory) brings home the fact that none of the perspectives suggested by sociologists have adequate explanatory power to delineate the facts that may go in articulating and managing social and economic inequalities in the Third World. The debates and counter debates on these perspectives have remained inconclusive. The gun or butter argument by scholars of development is that analyses of indigenous social structures of the developing nations including their political structures and the relationships of these nations (social, economic, cultural, political and military) with the developed nations, through development oriented bureaucracy and local leadership along with participation of people to relate development initiatives to their needs and aspirations, should form the basis of a "paradigm" for the development of these nations. This brings into focus the participatory model of development for the developing nations as the earlier prospectives on development have provided only privileged roles to the national elites.

Research evidence suggests that both the "Modernization" paradigm (capitalist model of development) and the neo-Marxist political economy model of development (socialist model) have failed to tackle the problem of poverty, unemployment and income disparities in the developing nations. In fact, these models of development have contributed to additional problems such as population growth, health and environmental hazards, malnutrition, child labour, delinquency, growth of slums, social tensions and agrarian unrest, ethnic rifts and strifes, labourers' and workers' agitations and a host of other social evils such as dowry, divorce, drug addiction, alcoholism, prostitution, etc. There is also an increase in the exploitation and oppression of backward class people, Scheduled Castes and Scheduled Tribes by the upper castes and classes in the Indian context.

While the "Modernization" paradigm has belied the trickle down approach of the capitalist, the socialist model has promoted coercion, force, stunting of freedom and mal-development of personality through heavy state interventions. Further, it has fostered favouritism and corruption.

In the wake of above experiences, one is tempted to examine the relevance of a participatory model of development in the context of developing nations. In this model, "people" have to be set in the centre of development. Within the cultural perspective, people's needs, aspirations, motivations and intentions have to be given the uppermost considerations. This will require evaluating the value preferences of the people although it is a tremendous task to have an assessment of the people's preferred social activities. Basically, this perspective on development should focus on the empowerment of people especially the weaker sections to enable them to initiate actions on their own so that they could influence the processes and outcomes of the development. Besides, there is a need of building social psychological capacities of the people so that they could take upon themselves the responsibility of managing the development schemes in a more effective and efficient manner. Felt needs of the people should be given priority over the real needs of the planners and the beginning can be made on tackling the overlapping needs, that is, the needs that overlap the felt and real needs. People need to be involved not only in the designing but in the implementation of the development schemes to promote agreement, cooperation and interaction not only in between the beneficiaries but between them and the implementation agencies so that delays are reduced, better service output is achieved and costs are minimized (Paul, 1987).

Three steps have been suggested in evolving a strategy of participation of the people in the development initiatives. First, there is an urgent need for conscintization of people through information sharing and consultations. A large segment of the population, especially from the weaker sections, have absolutely no idea of the type of problems that need developmental attention and tackling. They need to be made aware, conscious and given relevant information and knowledge for asserting their voices and making suitable demands through appropriate means on the governing and implementing agencies.

Secondly, there is a strong need to involve people in various decisions on specific issues related to development initiatives. Decision-making is a complex issue and whether taken at the individual or collective level always takes into account the maximum utilization expectation of people from the actions involved along with the likely consequences that may result from such action. Weighing of pros and cons related to actions, within the social organizational and value framework of the society, is highly desirable. This would warrant analysis of the societal or community social structure including power structure and leadership patterns; norms, values and sanctions which may retard or promote development initiatives or diffusion of innovations, existing channels of communication for transmitting information, removing doubts, apprehensions or misapprehensions and superstitions of people. Besides, social stratificational realities depicting poverty and affluence dimensions, influence patterns through caste and class affiliations, gender roles and equity dimensions need to be understood in totality along with land-labour arrangements and subsequent relationships. Family structure and religious adherences of the people also need to be analysed. A thorough analysis of the community social structure can go a long way in involving people and helping them to take decisions on the specific development schemes in relevance with their needs.

Thirdly, it is essential to have the institution-building process started at the community level so as to initiate action. Institution-building is not an easy task and it takes long to establish grassroot organisations through people's own initiative and their affirmative action to tackle a developmental issue or problem. A number of NGOs (Non-Governmental Organisations) over the years, have taken up responsibility of welfare of the people in the developing nations through their own initiative and action. In fact, in the recent past, there is rather an explosive emergence of NGOs as a major collective actor in development activities.

It is suggested that the invisible world of NGOs needs encouragement from the formal economic and political structures of the nation-State. The formal structures should not feel threatened by the emergence of these groups and wherever the spaces for economic and social development are visible, the NGOs should be encouraged to occupy them. Furthermore, it is argued that the mainstay of NGO's contribution to development is not as such financial as organisational, that is, NGOs are not required to financially induce development but to mobilize people into organised structures of group action. It is also pointed out that two fundamental actions in the development processes are local governments and local communities but bureaucracy and community are evidently two antithetical systems or styles of social organisations between the state and the poeple. Therefore, the alternative strategy to the governmental intervention is decentralization. Decentralization would encompass decentralization of power and authority, delegation to semi-autonomous or parastatal agencies, devolution of power to local government and transfer of functions from public to non-governmental institutions or joint exercise of both (Cernea, 1988).

However, the question often raised is, if centralization has failed in providing development, what is the guarantee that the decentralization process will hasten the progress of development. But, it is argued that it is only through the participation of the people in development activities that one can ensure their commitment to develop themselves as well as the community and to build up confidence in them to take decisions of their own. Centralized planning has resulted in creating greater dependency among the people. This has to be discouraged in order to develop self-reliance, which is fundamental for the progress of people in the developing countries (Mehta, 1984).

However, NGOs have been observed to suffer from certain handicaps. For example, they have limited replicability, self-sustainable technical capacity and lack broad programming context. However, they have the necessary capacity to outreach the inaccessible areas and the rural poor, besides promoting local participation. They are also in a position to operate on a low scale while innovating and adapting to the new settings and situations (Cernea, 1988).

People's organisations have to seek alternative ways of organising the society in order to manage our critically scarce resources as well as to have generation of values that guide our economic and political life. People have started to recognize their own worth and have explicitly contended that they should be allowed to fashion their own development processes. As such, they should be allowed to set their own agenda for development. The agenda should match with people's needs, aspirations and motivations. Poverty eradication, equitable distribution of resources, access to resources especially to the weaker sections, appropriate education, skill development, technological innovations, social and welfare services, should be the priority items on the agenda for development of the developing nations.

The essence of the participatory model of development is the mobilization, conscientization and organization of people. This process could act as a countervailing factor to ensuring greater social justice and equality for all. Further, epistemologically speaking, the growth of development theory and practice will occur in a dialectic fashion as at each stage, the lessons of practice will form the bases for further theory in this model of development (Wignaraja, 1991). Further, people-centred development should have human rights and democracy as a top priority on the development agenda of developing nations as these would encourage human dignity and enable people to participate fully in the affairs of the nations (Sasona and Serra, 1991). As such, a step towards social and cultural development will become conducive to economic development so necessary for human survival and well being. Media of communication can play a significant role in that direction. But, there is a need for democratization of media of communication for development purposes (Mehta, 1992).

In short, the participatory model of development is guided mainly by the etho-development perspective as well as by the development communication approach. In the etho-development perspective, people have to be placed in the centre stage of development and they have to be conscientized, organized mobilized and empowered to show commitment and responsibility towards themselves as well as towards others for building a self-reliant development strategy. The development communication strategy always acts as a catalyst to accelerate the development process of the people by creating a popular culture for development purposes and helping people to arrive at value consensus through resolutions of conflicts and tensions. Perhaps, in the context of developing nations, these perspectives should provide a better impetus to the development process than "the Modernization" paradigm or "dependency" or the "world system" theory.

Organization of the Material

As a development sociologist, I have traversed a long journey from village studies, agriculture and community development, through health and population, rural development to the academic of sociology. Having done fieldwork in different fields for nearly two decades, I gained insight into the processes and outcomes of development initiatives. The papers contained in this book are written after I have joined the academics. However, these are largely drawn in from the experiences I had in different development activities in different fields. As such, they provide a happy blend of theoretical formulations and practical applications in the sociology of development. This has been highlighted in chapter two.

To start with, the relevance of social theory in development planning has been highlighted. It is argued by some that conflict perspective drawn from Marxian ideology and interactionism as a part of interpretative sociology, are suitable for analysing and understanding development planning. However, it is contended that since sociology falls short of the expectations of physical or biological sciences, there is a need to consider all short or long term perspectives in sociology to comprehend the phenomenon of development planning.

This is followed by the role of a sociologist in the development initiatives. Based on my personal experience of having worked on a rural development project sponsored by the World Bank, in Mauritius, it is suggested that a sociologist, as a theoretician may be expected to diagnose or analyse the impediments to the development initiatives but as a practitioner of sociology, he or she should acquire an interventionist role to institute changes directed by the development initiatives into the community social structure.

Social change in the community follows the path of least resistance and is vulnerable to various types of resistances that may be inherent in the social structure. But in the process of social changes, development may cause various kinds of social tensions and unrest. The management of social tensions as a consequence of development activities, forms the subject matter of chapter four.

Five decades of development planning has not yielded the desired results. Development, by and large, remained lopsided and created islands of wealth in the vast ocean of poverty. There was a dusk of despair all around because of increased poverty, income disparities, unemployment, illiteracy, malnutrition and population rise. To have the dawn of hope, there is a need to go in for certain hard options to make development a reality in our setting. This has been highlighted while delineating various development perspectives having a bearing on our development strategy in chapter five.

Rural development is central to Indian situation. As such, development in India based on a case of rural development has been analysed within the structural-functional perspective, the premise being that Marxian perspective because of India's cultural and civilizational factors has a limited application. Some of the issues of sociological import associated with the rural development in India, have been highlighted in chapter six.

Development of a nation cannot be done in isolation from the other developed and developing nations. With market economic forces getting dominant in international trade relations and liberalization from trade and tariff controls, the process of globalization has set in and it improves upon the development of a developing nation as well. However, this globalization process, instead of homogenising the various nations into one world, has fractured them into many more parts due to resurgence of ethnicity and ethnicism. A value perspective advocating sharing of common values at the global level may be conducive for development of all. This is the subject matter of chapter seven.

India, as wedded to democracy, is acquiring its full potential and in view of the failure of the "Modernization" paradigm, has to evolve a "participatory" model of development and place 'people' in the entire development process. To sensitize people and to empower them with adequate knowledge and suitable skills to mould their own future, media of communication is required to play a significant role in the development. This aspect has been discussed in the subsequent two chapters. The conceptual and methodological issues related to communication and development form the subject matter of chapter eight while a suitable development communication. Strategy has been highlighted in the next chapter.

"Putting people First" in the development initiatives is not only desirable but is compelling in view of capitalist and socialist models of development having failed in achieving the set goals for India's development. The dynamics of development in the Indian society, factors retarding the development process over the last five decades have been highlighted and a "people centred" approach has been suggested in chapter ten.

Backwardness of communities in India's population is the most stumbling block in their development. An increasing rise of population in them further make them prove to poverty. In such a situation it is debatable whether, our nation can move towards a civil society or not. These issues have been discussed in chapter eleven.

Quite lately, the development paradigm has started including the element of sustainability of activities because of limited resources on the planet and overexploitation of the same for the development of the developed and the developing nations. In the light of this hue and cry for the development of the present, without affecting the future generations, the possibility of attaining sustainable development in the wake of poverty and population growth in our country, has been discussed in the context of changing social structure in chapter twelve.

In the final analysis, the social aspects of development especially in the context of our nation, have been highlighted. Apart from theoretical formulations, the dynamics of interacting variables in our setting have also been gives to make development a social reality for a developing nation.

References

Amin, Semir, (1976), *Unequal Development: An essay on the social formulation of peripheral capitalism*, Hassocks, Harvester.

Baran, Paul, (1973), *The Political Economy of Growth*, Harmondsworth, Penguin Press.

Batubennga, Nkashama, (1993), Rome, "Reconsidering the concept "Development", *Development*, Journal of the Society for

International Development, Vol. 2, p. 26.

Carmen, Raff, (1994), "Development Ethics, Rome or the Rediscovery and Reclamation of Meaning", *Development*, Journal of the Society for International Development, Vol. 4, pp. 17-24.

Cernea, Michael M., (1988), *Non-Governmental Organizations and Local Development*, Washington D.C., The World Bank (Agriculture and Rural Development Department).

Cernea, Michael M., (1997), "Eight Main Risks' Impoverishment and Social Justice in Population Resettlement" in *Poverty, Population and Sustainable Development* (ed.) Mehta, S.R., Jaipur, Rawat Publications.

Frank, A.G., (1978), *Dependent Accumulation and Underdevelopment*, London, MacMillan.

Frank, Andre Gundre, (1969), *Latin America: Underdevelopment or Revolution*, New York, Monthly Review Press.

Hagen, E., (1960), *On the Theory of Social Change*, Homewood Illinois, Dossey Press.

Harrison, David, (1989), *The Sociology of Modernization and Development*, New Delhi, Heritage Publishers.

Hoselitz, B., (1960), *Sociological Aspects of Economic Growth*, New York, Free Press.

Inayatullah, Sohail, (1994), "Beyond, Development and towards Prama", Rome, *Development*, Journal of the Society for International Development, p. 24.

Inkles, A., and Smith, D.H., (1974), *Becoming Modern, Cambridge*, Mass, Harvard University Press.

Lerner, Daniel, (1958), *The Passing of the Traditional Society*, New York, Free Press.

Maxneef, Manfred, A., (1990), "Notes on the Semiology of our Mega crisis", *Development*, Rome, Journal of the Society for International Development, 3/4.

McClelland D.C., (1961), *The Achieving Society*, New York, Free Press.

Mehta, S.R., (1972), *Emerging Pattern of Rural Leadership*, New Delhi, Wiley Eastern Pvt. Ltd.

Mehta, S.R., (1981), *Social Development in Mauritius: A Study of Rural Modernization of an Island Community*, New Delhi, Wiley Eastern Ltd.

Mehta, S.R., (1984), *Rural Development Policies and Programmes: A Sociological Perspective*, New Delhi, Sage Publications Pvt. Ltd.

Mehta, S.R., (1992) (ed.), *Communication and Development: Issues and Perspectives*, Jaipur, Rawat Publications.

Mehta, S.R., (1997) (ed.), *Poverty, Population and Sustainable Development: Essays in honour of Professor V.S. D'Souza*, Jaipur, Rawat Publications.

Myrdal, Gunnar, (1970), *An approach to the Asian Drama: Methodological and Theoretical*, Vintage Books.

Parsons, Talcott, (1964), "Evolutionary Universals in Society", *American Sociological Review*, 29 (3), June, pp. 339-57.

Paul, Samuel, (1987), *Community Participation in Development Projects: The World Bank Experience*, Washington D.C., The World Bank.

Portes, Alejandro and Jolu Walton, (1981), *Labour, Class and the International System*, New York, Academic Press.

Portes, Alejandro, (1997), "Neoliberalism and the Sociology of Development". *Population and Development Review*, Vol. 23, No. 2 (June).

Roberts, Bryan R., (1978), *Cities of Peasants: The Political Economy of Urbanization in the Third World*, London. Edward Arnold.

Rostow, W.W., (1960), *The Stages of Economic Growth: A non-Communist Manifesto*, London, Cambridge University Press.

Sasona, Adi and Angela Mia Serra, (1991), "A People's Development Agenda for the 1990's", *Development*, Rome, Journal of the Society for International Development.

Servaes, Jan., (1986), "Communication and Development Paradigms: An Overview". *Media Asia*, Vol. 13, No. 3.

Smelser, Neil, (1965), *The Sociology of Economic Life*, New Delhi, Prentice Hall of India.

Wallerstein, I. (1979), *The Capitalist World Economy*, Cambridge: Cambridge University Press.

Weber, Max, (1930), *The Protestant Ethic and the Spirit of Capitalism*, London, Allen and Unwin.

White, Robert A., (1990), "Cultural Analysis in Communication for Development—The Role of Cultural Dramaturgy in the Creation of a Public Sphere", *Development*, Rome, Journal of the Society for International Development.

Wignaraja Poona, (1991), "Participatory Development, Growth and Equity: No Trade Offs". *Development*, Rome, Journal of the Society for International Development.

2

Development, Planning and Social Theory

Sociologists have often been dubbed by policy planners and administrators as those dealing with the "obvious." This type of reaction has cast a shadow on the status of sociology in certain circles. One prime reason for this, is that sociologists often agree to participate in the solution of problems which lack precise and clearcut definitions. Further, some sociologists subscribe to rhetorical ideology, and do not give in easily to pre-existing solutions conceived by the planners (Bailey, 1975). This position of sociology (and sociologists) warrants a closer look at conceptual and methodological issues related to development and the relevance of social theory to planning. The present attempt is an effort in this direction.

Development is usually treated as a generic term connoting growth, evolution, stage of inducement or progress. The concept of development got currency after the Second World War. Economists operationalize development as growth in per capita Gross National Product (or a similar national accounts figure). A large number of developing countries have failed to achieve a satisfactory rate of growth of per capita GNP in the last five decades. Observers of the developing world have concluded that this has been due to insufficient attention given to social and political factors in planning (Galnoor, 1971). On the contrary, some scholars believe that planning as such, is inimical to development and a need for planning occurs only at the crisis management level (Dror, 1965). They believe that "non-scientific" vision is a better guide to development planning; "there is no use in being systematic about nation building which is, almost, by definition unsystematic" (Galnoor, 1971).

But experience with development planning has shown that intuitive, ad hoc decisions are not profitable and that development plans have to be conceived or designed on a well-informed basis. This highlights, further, the significance of a need for a new conceptualization of development.

Development means different things to different people. Laufer, states, "It means dams and factories, roads and canals, bush clearing, electrification, soil improvement, universities, secondary schools, primary schools, sanitation, research and a multitude of other activities and achievements. But, above all, development means people—The preparation and activation of people is the cause of economic and social development" (Laufer, 1967). For others, "national development objectives relate not only to a rate of growth, but also to income distribution and other social goals" (Hirchman, 1965).

GNP or consumption per head does not measure what sociologists are interested in, namely the conditions in which people live. It is clear that the same goods and services may have very different effects on different people under varying circumstances. Secondly, wastage of various kinds occurring at the production, marketing or consumption stage, are often not accounted for in the national plans. Thirdly, due to maldistribution, the goods and services produced may not generate welfare for a large proportion of the population. And finally, some aspects of welfare (like leisure), the feeling of security and the like are not reflected in the national accounting. (Rodan, 1969). It has been emphasized that "apart from the economic problems" of producing goods and services, we have the "social problems" of using those resources in such a way as to improve the welfare effect of the economic activity (Drewinski 1971). Thus the social indicators of development should always be considered alone with the economic ones. That is why, of late, it has been stated that development is not to be measured in terms of growth only but it is explicitly expressed as "Social Change" plus "Growth." The element of change has brought along with it the process of structural differentiation, integration and social disturbances in the institutional set-ups for a new social order (Smelser, 1965). Thus the qualitative changes occur concurrently along with the quantitative change (Colm and Greiger, 1965). Development in the new perspective has been referred to as an overall process of transforming Men and societies leading to a social order in which every human being can achieve moral and material well-being.,

Development has also been referred to as an integral, value loaded cultural process encompassing the natural environment, social relations, education, production and consumption and well being (FAO). .The "Study Guide on Development" of the Food and Agricultural Organization, for example, states that "the ultimate purpose of development is to provide everyone with ever increasing opportunities for a better life. It therefore, requires an equitable distribution of income and other social resources in order to promote justice and efficient production, to raise the level of employment substantially, to expand and improve facilities for education, health, nutrition, housing, social and cultural well-being. The qualitative and structural changes that development thus imposes on society must go in hand with economic progress while racial, ethnic and social inequalities must be substantially reduced. These are decisive factors in hastening development and hence must be handled with dynamism" (FAO, 1975).

The urgency of development is ubiquitous. It lies in the poverty of the masses of the developing nations as well as that of others whose basic human needs like food, cloth, shelter, medical facilities, and education are not met. It also lies, in a large part of the world, in the alienation of the masses both in misery and in affluence who are deprived of the means to understand and master their social and political environment. It is also said that there is a growing feeling of frustration that disturbs the industrialized societies (Development Dialogue, 1975). But the solution to these crises has to be an endogeneous one. Development should spring from the heart of each society which "relies first on its own strength and resources and defines its sovereignty, the vision of its future, cooperating with societies sharing its problems and aspirations." (Development Dialogue, 1975) Self-reliance is the key to development especially for the developing countries. The developed nations should nevertheless shoulder a major responsibility and fulfil a moral obligation to help the developing world with technical and financial resources for bettering their environment and for further expansion of their indigenous resources.

In the developing countries, development has to be considered as a social and cultural changes as well as economic growth and these changes can concomitantly affect the attitudes, motives, values and norms of the members of a society for a new social order. The politico-social, technical and economic changes are so interrelated with each other that it is difficult to separate one from the other (Hagen, 1965). In this context, the concept of development should be viewed both from the evolutionary and revolutionary perspectives of social change.

Evolution is conceived of as a process of growth, increasing complexity, increasing differentiation of structure and function and increasing interdependence among the differentiated parts of the social system. In terms of economic development, the rates of growth are determined to a large extent by the factors of production like national resources, capital investment, labour entrepreneurial talent which in turn are conditioned by savings, inflation, balance of payments, foreign aid, size of population and rate of population change (Burton, 1961). The doctrine of evolution has been to give legitimization to the nation of an automatic and wholesale progress in human affairs. But progress depends not on the existence of social change but on the direction which human beings deliberately bring to that change. The root meaning of progress is "to go forward" but when considered as a quality of social change or evolution, progress can hardly be defined. At best, it can only be described or characterized. Progress is an evaluative concept which denotes change for the better whether cultural elements considered are material or non-material. Progress is also purely subjective and exists only in the mind of the observer.

On the other hand, a revolution brings in rapid and fundamental alterations in the institutions of a society and of its power distribution. It is often rapid and discontinuous in form and is likely to involve violence but may well be orderly as opposed to erratic (Smelser, 1965). Sorokin opines that revolutions are most probably the transitional periods with respect to major cultural values and are fundamental bases of social relationship (Sorokin, 1957). A necessary though not sufficient condition for revolution is a deterioration in one or another of the major meaningful aspects of human "Welfare"

(Moore, 1965). One of the great advocates of the revolutionary change is Marx (Aron, 1965) who presented a series of changes at the structural level in his analysis of the evolution from feudalism through capitalism to communism. According to him, advancement towards a classless society proceeds through "dialectical" conflicts, in each of which one subordinate class overthrows its ruling class in order to establish a new order in the society. This historical perspective of economic analysis is not in vogue with the modern economists who tend to measure the progress of a nation in terms of quantitative indicators. It is well-known that there is hardly a single theory coherent in nature that could explain the phenomenon of social change. Grand theories of evolutionary or neo-evolutionary schools or that of conflict school of thought, have highlighted different aspects of the phenomenon of social change but we have yet to find a satisfactory explanation.

Before briefly analysing the evolutionary and revolutionary theories of social change, it may be important to understand the concept of social change. This concept has been defined by different scholars but it could be taken to mean simply the process of becoming different in any sense, that is bio-physical social, cultural, economic, psychological and political aspects of human life. In other words, it could mean a change in size, magnitude, or alteration in structure or function of a given system. More defines it as "the significant alterations of social structure, that is, of patterns of social action and interaction, including consequences and manifestations of such structures embodied in norms, values and cultural products and symbols (Moore, 1965). He further contends that "since there is no singular theory of social structure in more than a differential sense, there is no reason to expect a singular theory of change, since different types of social organizations set different variables for analysing changes in patterns of actions (Moore, 1967). In the context of the planned programmes, we are mainly concerned with planned change or purposeful change. This has been defined as "increase in control over the conditions of existence" or alternatively as "an expansion of resources" (Coleman, 1971). This concept of social change is close to that of social development.

Development, Planning and Social Theory

It is observed that commitment to development is a commitment to the future. Progress does not happen itself but it can be made to happen. This necessitates building a kind of attitude that should view the future as a possibility through the control and manipulation of the environment. Efficiency is an estimate of those in power to affect or bring about a desired future state. Planning has been considered as an organized intelligent attempt to select the best possible alternative to achieve specific goals (Waterston, 1965). Nehru, for example, stated that planning is an exercise of intelligence to deal with facts and situations as they are and find a way to solve problems. (Nehru on Planning)

The goal of development planning is growth plus change. Accelerated economic growth and structural change are the two main aims of planning. Development planning may be defined as an organized action by the State to raise the rate of socio-economic growth in order to provide better living conditions for its citizens. The plans also seek to alter institutional arrangements which are considered to be hurdles in the accomplishment of these goals. Thus a plan may include a number of programmes with detailed determination of specific objectives to be achieved within each sector and region in accordance with a specified time schedule (Colm and Geiger, 1962).

In developed countries, economic analysis needs to concern itself explicitly with economic manifestations, already embodying the outcome of the operations of complex social, political, psychological and other non-economic factors. On the other hand, economic analysis in the underdeveloped countries do not incorporate non-economic factors in their models of development because such factors do not conform to the conventional western theories. In this connection, Waterstone, states, "If there is something in the nature of conventional planning or in the milieu of the low income countries, which make it unrealistic to expect the responses required for successful operation of conventional planning in these countries, it may be more sensible to try, at least, at first to modify the theory rather than the responses of political leaders" (Waterston,

1969). The models of development should, therefore, include the statement of clear objectives within the constraints of operative ideology, the availability of resources and planned techniques of their mobilization.

The main components of development planning are : (1) objectives, goals and targets (2) resources (3) selection of means to mobilize resources (4) formulation of specific programme and (5) provision of its implementation. Operationally speaking, planning consists of two processes, from the "top-down" and from the "bottom-up". While the planning authorities are engaged mostly in the "top down process," they should also attempt to follow the "bottom-up" procedure in the development process. A number of data on population, labour, production, production of gas and electricity, agriculture, forestry, fishing, mining, manufacturing, construction, wholesale, retail and related service trades, transportation, education, health and other welfare services, external trade, money and banking, finance and general prices, government and personal incomes and conditions of living is required for development, planning (Colm and Geiger, 1962). Waterston states that planning in most less developed countries is severely handicapped by a widespread lack of information (Waterston, 1969). Besides, there are shortages in resources, skilled personnel and leaders who want to use a broad range of information. In addition, there are social and cultural barriers to economic progress inherent in the traditional structure, value system and absence of creativity that offer difficulties in the implementation of plans in these countries.

There is a linkage suggested between ideology and development planning. It is stated that "no action at all is possible without ideological underpinning and we cannot adequately chose between alternative actions without an understanding of the nature of beliefs that make them" (Bailey, 1975). Merton has suggested that the intention in the usage of this term (ideology) is to ascribe motive to particular people and groups of people which do not stem from desire for some independent cognitive truth but derive from interest (Merton, 1972). This intellectual interest is reflected in seeing the world that conforms to a preexisting idea held about it, an idea of which one has become convinced of independently of the evidence. Bailey suggests that this may appear to be contradicting rather than contrasting to the scientific approach in the whole problem of planning but "the supposed antagonism between ideology and science is a false one." He contends that "if we idealize everything, then science has to provide the criterion of truthful knowledge. As such, science is an ideology and the scientific ideology would involve one in applying a method both applicable to the physical and to the social world" (Bailey, 1975). Thus the planning process has to take into account the belief system, the subjects like social classes, planners, political parties, etc., and the objects like housing, transport welfare, efficiency, etc., on a well-informed basis, and this scientific approach has to make a critical use of the sociology of knowledge. Further, it may be emphasized that the application of social theory to the development planning will have to be considered in the context of political stability or instability of a nation. Political instability may be reckoned with as a factor significant enough to retard the development process in the developing countries. There is a high degree of political competitiveness and the degree of economic development (Almond and Coleman, 1960). In certain situations, economic growth itself is a cause of political instability. In socialist countries, drastic institutional arrangements were altered to remove political, economic and social conditions influencing their backwardness in order to achieve a high level of growth in production and income. In countries with a mixed economy, however, institutional change also takes precedence over económic progress (Hoselitz, 1961).

All economic phenomena are social phenomena and both of these together make a social reality. It should be stressed that in order to reduce social inequalities in income as well as in cultural and political fields, it is necessary to improve all possible forms of social and political participation. In the developing countries, attention must be given equally to both the urban and the rural sectors which already differ in relation to employment, information, education and voting (Waterston, 1965).

Two paradigms of economic development have been suggested by the development planners (Weaver, 1975). The basic paradigm of traditional economics, based on the concept of the "economic Man" stresses the goal of the maximum consumption of goods and services with minimum efforts. It is assumed that as development proceeds, the capitalist will reinvest and will employ more persons and this will help in the redistribution of income among a large segment of the population. But this "grow now" and "trickle later" approach has failed to tackle the problems of unemployment, inequality of income, regional disparities and the dilemma of poverty, malnutrition and the illiteracy fully in the developing nation of the Third World. Currently, they advocate the working for a standard of living for the developing nations in consistency with their own resources and with their own values. It is being stressed that basic human needs should be given priority over demand items of luxury. Planning for production and distribution should be done simultaneously and the poor should be provided with means so that they can satisfy their needs. A greater stress on labour rather than on capital intensive projects is being made to tackle the problem of unemployment. The other paradigm of economic, development is historical and holistic and is advocated by political economists. Their goal of development is based on the liberation of a nation within as well as liberation from its position of subordination and dependency from the rich developed nations. Social ownership, centralized planning to allocate the factors of production, land, labour, capital and directing social surplus into the productive investments in order to meet people's basic needs, are the measures suggested for development purposes; social revolution is considered to be a prerequisite for development.

Whatever be the strategy or model of development, one thing is certain that one cannot ignore the significance of social, cultural and political factors for the development of the poor nations. In these nations, economic liberation and an integrated social life should be the two main objectives of development. The methods of development should be designed in consonance with the need structure and value pattern of the people in these countries. A vast majority of the population in these nations live in rural areas and is below the absolute poverty line, as such, their development would lie only in raising the income level of these people to a certain level of living, through the careful design of inputs. This economic emancipation shall help them to enhance their social status or prestige in the community's evaluation of them and they will become more self-reliant and self-sustaining (Mehta, 1981). Land is a limiting factor with most of these nations and there is a need to bring in the non-agricultural or industrial sector as close as possible to this rural areas. This will help to diversify occupation and thereby break up the social solidarities like caste or kinship ties impeding the development process. With the political ideals of democracy it wouldn't be possible to make land available to all, even with the best of land tenure laws and land ceilings; as such industrial development must supplement the agricultural development. Even the bringing of the non-agricultural sector closer to the rural population would usher in infrastructure facilities and social amenities which have for long been the privilege of urban people; it would check migrations from rural to urban centres and build up more integrated living patterns. Appropriate technology should reduce the regional, social and economic disparities. Further participation of people in the development process is essential and this should be accelerated through the local political, economic and social institutions. If denied, this would liquidate democracy and its ideals could get replaced by the non-democratic forces in due course of time. This will then call forth a different strategy of development.

As regards the indicators of development, although it may be possible to develop hard indicators for economic development, yet the indicators for social development are likely to be descriptive-cum-analytical because of the softness of data in most cases. There are different indicators to be employed at societal, community and individual levels (Mehta, 1981). Some of the broad indicators of development at the societal level could be economic growth, industrialization, urbanization, literacy rate, employment status, agricultural development, health status, improved means of communication, technological advancement, the development of art and culture, the scientific and rational outlook of people, stable political institutions and the legitimization of social action appropriate to the need structure of the people. At the community level the development could be visualized in terms of the mobility of individuals or groups in the social hierarchy, the standard of living of people, the involvement and participation of leadership and organization in community, decision making, increased employment opportunities, the provision of infrastructure amenities like health centre, market, welfare centre, school, post office and telephone, improved roads and paths, the mechanization of farms, the development of basic industries, a decline in crime rates and collective and rational efforts to solve the problems of the community. The possession of material objects by the individual families, the construction of new houses, public lavatories, bus shelters, playgrounds, improved means of communications, migrations and the politicization of social and economic groups may be other indicators of development at the community level. The development at the individual level is reflected by a more rational or scientific outlook, attitudes, values and norms conducive to modernization of groups or communities.

In regard to the relevance of social theory in development planning, critiques of different perspectives in sociology have been made by scholars to highlight the relevance of one perspective over other. It is argued that the absolutist scientific approach advocated by system theorists, based on "value consensus" perspective is deterministic and present only a monolithic social structure for society. Further, interpretative sociologist of the symbolic interactionists' school, phenomenologists and ethnomethodologists are critical of the system theory because (a) structural theories can only explain very broadly, described categories of behaviours and (b) structural theory denies intentionality, choice, freedom in any important way that should mark it off from positivism. According to them, society is composed of social relationships which are made rather than structures which just exist and grow and Men are seen to interpret the world rather than to react to it (Bailey, 1975). But it has been seen that people are to a large extent also influenced by the structures of which they are the part. The limitation of explaining all social phenomena especially behaviour and attitude by the character of social institutional structure and concomitant institutional values of functionalism and systems theory and ignoring the fact that people are influenced by the structures, by the ethnomethodologists, has led to a renewed interest in the conflict perspective. It is mainly concerned with analysing power as the structural property and showing a concern for action and social change. This perspective views Man as a potentially free actor whose freedom has been repressed by the manipulative social institutions but this condition is "historical" rather than "natural" and therefore, can be changed. In this background, Bailey suggests that there are two kinds of phenomena, Man as a meaning-creating being, and society as a structure of rival power groups, that the interpretative and conflict social theories become appropriate for planning. (Bailey, 1975) But empirical evidence does suggest that some of the other sociological perspectives also provide an understanding of the development process. The topologists among sociologists have done much to improve our understanding of the whole process of urbanization. In addition, such an approach to community has shown that one of the chief barriers to rapid economic, political or health change is the traditionalism in the values found in the folk, peasant or rural communities. System theory and functionalism have shown that every society and community consists of interlocking and interrelated institutions, organizations or groupings and change in one will affect changes in other spheres (Burgess, 1963). This has been significant since this has helped the planners to advocate an integrated rather than segmented approach in development projects.

To sum up, one says that social theory is not so exact as to match with the scientific criteria of the physical sciences but efforts are towards building a reasonable approximation and better understanding of social events or actions on the basis of analytical frames through a diagnostic approach. Social theory can become a useful analytical tool for diagnosing problems, but so far as social engineering is concerned it shall have to be supplemented by other social and management sciences. Human action or behaviour is complex and is at variance with different situations; as such, all social and psychological perspectives having any bearing on it will have relevance for planned development of the developing nations. The development planners cannot and should not ignore these along with economic factors.

References

Almond, G.A., Coleman James S., et al. (1960), *The Politics of Developing Areas*, Princeton : Princeton University Press.

Aron, Raymond, (1965), *Main Currents in Sociological Thought* (Karl Marx), Volume I (Penguin Books), pp. 111-82.

Bailey, Joe, (1975), "Interpretative Sociology," *Social Theory for Planning, op. cit.* pp. 88-104.

Bailey, Joe, (1975), *Social Theory for Planning*, London; Routledge Kegan Paul, p. 1.

Burgess, M. Elaine, (1963), "The Sociologist Looks at Community and Community Development," *Community Development Seminar*, University of North Carolina, School of Public Health, (May 5-9).

Burton, Henry J, (1961), "Contemporary Theorizing on Economic Growth" in Bert F. Hostelitz (ed.) *Theories of Economic Growth* Glencoe, Illinois : The Free Press.

Coleman, James S., (1971), "Conflicting Theories of Social Change." *American Behavioural Scientist* (14 : 5 May and June).

Colm, 'Gerhard and Geiger, Theodre, (1965) "Country Programming as a Guide to Development" in Robert E. Asher and Others (eds.). *Development of Emerging Countries: An Agendu for Research* Washington, D.C : Brokings Institutions.

Drewniwski Jan, (1971), "The Practical Significance of Social Information", *Annals of the American Academy of Political and Social Sciences* (January), p. 84.

Dror Bengemin Akzinand Yehazket, (1966), *Israel: High Pressure Planning*, Syracuse, N.Y : Syracuse University Press.

Food and Agriculture Organisation of the United Nations, Rome, *Study Guide on Development*, Freedom from Hunger Campaign/Action for Development, p. 5.

Galnoor, Itzhak, "Social Information for What" *Annals of the American Academy of Political and Social Sciences, (January)*

Hagen E. Everett, (1965), "A Framework for Analysing Economic and Political Change," in Robert C. Asher and others, *op. cit.*

Hirschman, Albert, (1965), "Obstacles to Development: A classification and quasi vanishing Act," *Economic Development and Cultural Change* (13 July), pp. 385-93.

Hoselitz, B.F., (1961), "Theories of Stages of Economic Growth" in B.F. Hoselitz. (ed.) *Theories of Economic Growth*, Gleucoe, Illinois : The Free Press.

Laufer, Leopold, (1967), *Israel and the Developing Countries: New Approaches to Co-operation*, New York : Twentieth Century Fund, p. 69.

Mehta, S.R., (1981), *Social Development in Mauritius*, New Delhi : Wiley Eastern Ltd., p. 156.

Merton, R.K., (1972), "Insiders and Outsiders: A Chapter in the Sociology of Knowledge" *American Journal of Sociology* (78), pp. 1-8.

Moore, Wilbert E., (1967), *Order and Change,* New York : John Wiley and Sons, p. 3.

Moore, Wilbet E., (1965), *Social Change,* New Delhi : Prentice Hall of India, p. 82.

Nehru, Jawaharlal, *Strategy of the Third Plan* (New Delhi : Planning Commission), pp. 33-34.

Rodan, Resenstein, (1969), "Criteria for Evaluation of National Development Effort" *Journal of Development Planning* (1), p. 5.

Smelser, Neil, J., (1965), *The Sociology of Economic Life,* New Delhi: Prentice-Hall of India.

Sorokin, P. (1957), *Social and Cultural Dynamics,* Boston : Porter Sargent.

The 1975 Dag Hammerskjold Report on Development and International Cooperation, "Introduction–to set in motion the process of change." *Development Dialogue* (No. 1/2, 1975), p. 5.

Waterston, Albert, (1965), *Development Planning: Lessons of Experience,* Baltimore, Maryland : The Johns Hopkins Press.

Waterston, Albert, (1969), "An Operational Approach to Development Planning." Paper presented at a conference of the *Crisis in Planning* at the University of Sussex, England, p. 3.

Weaver, James H., (1975), "Economic Development of Two Paradhigms" *Development Studies Programme,* Agency for International Development Washington D.C. Transcript of talk (May).

3

A Sociologist/An Anthropologist in the Development Initiatives

Development Perspectives

As a developmental anthropologist, I had a unique opportunity of associating myself as an evaluator in The World Bank sponsored project on Rural Development in Mauritius, for nearly five years. This provided me with many gainful insights into the ongoing development processes in a developing nation of tiny size. The replication of some of these experiences in the context of development of a country of continental size such as India, may appear inappropriate but it definitely provides some clues that may have bearing on the development of any developing nation.

As a part of the project, while on a mission to The World Bank, Washington D.C., we visited Harvard Institute for International Development, Harvard University (USA). The core faculty of this institute was a group of economists who expressed surprise and despair in the appointment of a Sociologist (myself) on a Development Project. As an expatriate sociologist, responsible for the evaluation of this project, I felt dismayed at this reaction to begin with, but soon mustered courage to retort "Why, is development the prerogative of economists only?"

This anecdotal narration may sound superficial to many but for me, it was a grand learning experience. Development till lately was considered as an exclusive domain of economists. It is only recently that the implementation of development programmes in the developing nations has thrown up a series of new socio-political configurations. These have not been understood by various economic perspectives and that is why, the sociological standpoint now gets recognized. This bringing in of non-economic factors to the forefront has necessitated in conceiving development as growth plus social and cultural change (Mehta, 1981).

GNP or consumption per head does not measure what we as sociologists are interested in-namely, the conditions in which people lie. Development has to be considered as a dynamic concept of a stable society and within the framework of growth plus change, accelerated economic growth and structural change become its expressed or implied aims (Mehta, 1984).

Development has been described as a generic term meaning growth, evolution, stage of inducement or progress (Mehta, 1981). Herbert Spenser conceived development of society as a process of evolution. Like an organic evolution, it is a process of growth, increasing complexity of units, increasing inter-dependence among the differentiated parts and that of industrial order establishing global community. Similarly, August Comta emphasized, three stages of developments—theological metaphysical and positivism. Marxist theory of society is also basically a theory of progress, though not of linear type. Advancement towards the classless society proceeds through dialectical conflicts, in each of which one subordinate class overthrows its ruling class only to establish a new order and this process of development continues. Max Weber provides a cyclical approach to development while conveiving history as more open to human guidance. Man is caught into his own created institutional web but at charismatic moments, he breaks in, remodelling the institutional structure to bring it closer to his wish or design. This routinization of charisma follows a cyclical path in the development process. On cultural level, Weber views that increased rationalization would indicate increased submission of the nature to Man's mind (Etzioni and Etzioni, 1964).

These classical theories of evolution, advancement and progress were not appreciated by the modern economists and they tended to view development of a society more in terms of economic growth expressed as GNP or per captia income or as any other national accounting figure. It is argued that this concept of development grew out of certain historical events, such as the Industrial Revolution in Europe and the United

States, the colonial experience in Latin America, Africa and Asia, the quantitative empiricism of North American Social Science and capitalistic economic/political philosophy. This model of development remained in practice till about 1970s, when scholars started doubting the ideology of development of traditional societies into modern ones as a part of contemporary intellectual extension of social Darwinian evolution as well as that of treating the developed nations of the West as the ideal towards which the developing nations should move (Rogers, 1976).

In view of this model of development showing disgusting results in the case of developing nations, there were efforts made to look for development concepts and methods in congruence with the needs and value orientation of the developing nations. The sudden opening of international relations with China further helped in gaining insights into its path of development.

The alternative model of development emphasized on equality of distribution, concern with quality of life, integration of "traditional" and "modern" system in a country, intermediate level and labour intensive technology, self-reliance in development, popular participation in decentralized self-development planning and execution and on the internal and external causes of underdevelopment as against economic growth, capital intensive technology, centralized planning and on the internal causes of underdevelopment envisaged in the previously held dominant model of development.

This expanded concept of development, with its builtin flexibility and humanitarian orientation provides larger canvas to sociologists and social anthropologists for their intervention in the development planning, implementation and evaluation of plans, programmes or projects. These terms have been used interchangeably in this paper. The main difference between them is in terms of extent of specificity of objectives. For example, Gunnar Myrdal in his Asian Drama, emphasized on institutions and attitudes in the development of developing nations. These have to be considered not in isolation but in their mutual relationships. Further, the identification of target areas and target groups not only helped the intended beneficiaries of the developmental inputs but it also highlighted the concept of "putting people first" in the development milieu. Gandhian philosophy of Man in relation to Society also focuses on satisfaction of basic human needs rather than greed, treating work not as a disutility but as a fulfilment of personality, decentralization of government and on a technology which serves social needs. The neo-Marxians or radical economists have also considered underdevelopment of the developing nations as a consequence of capitalist path of development. They advocate replacement of old institution by the creation of new structures of power favouring the poor as a result of conflicts generated within the society (Parthasarathy, 1982).

Frank, favours for a world economic order which he expects to be uneven and also for social revolution in the developing nations for a change in their conditions of life, yet he expresses with despair that the international capitalist economic system has become so powerful that the periphery countries cannot escape the dominance of core countries for their development, so much so that even some of the socialist countries which should have moved to the next stage of communism, are getting back to the capitalist path of development (Frank, 1983).

An overview of development perspectives makes one believe that development is a more difficult and challenging proposition. Rene' Dubos, the French Ecologist's proverbial expression, "Think globally but act locally" draws one's attention to conceive development as an overall process of transforming Men and Societies to a social order in which every human being may be able to achieve moral and material well being in consistence with one's own values and traditions. As a sequel to this, I have argued in my study on Rural Development that economic development cannot take place without a change in the value system and social organization of the people in our villages. The institutional, technological infrastructural participative and human development service oriented changes have been suggested to affect the village social structure in terms of occupational diversification, social mobility, reduction in income disparities and changes in values and social relationships for an integrated social living. These changes can be effected through decentralized planning and the consequent involvement and commitment of community leaders (Mehta, 1984).

Anthropological Interventions

In the present context, the terms social anthropology and sociology will be used interchangeably as both deal with people, their cultures and societies. However, the strength of social anthropology lies in its inductive approach, that is inferring general laws from particular instances, found effective for the delineation of cultural and social processes of community structures and subcultures at a particular time. The sociologists, on the other hand, employ a deductive-inductive approach for the validation of their concepts. But what is important is to identify the entrance points for the sociological or anthropological know-how into the development milieu of environment.

Development would imply planned intervention to bring in a desirable change in a particular direction. As such, the development planning would envisage a cycle of setting goals and targets, determination and mobilization of resources, formulation of specific programmes, designing of implementation strategy and evaluation of efforts and activities. At each level, anthropological or sociological know-how can contribute meaningfully and an anthropologist as a member of development planning team can provide interventions suitable to the accomplishment of programme goals.

Development planning process would involve tackling the national problems on regional and sectoral basis. Anthropologists are considered specialists in tackling the welfare problems and administration of tribals and backward class people in regional development projects and schemes for them. But quite lately, their interventions in development plans, programmes or projects in sectoral developments related to areas such as Agriculture, Industry, Health, Population Control, Education, etc., are being appreciated by the planners and administrators of the developing nations, in view of focus on "putting people first".

Apart from their involvement in rural development, an increasing number of anthropologists, especially in the West, are getting involved in urban development as well. However, the most unfortunate part is that the involvement of an anthropologist or a sociologist is at the evaluation stage of the development project; to find out whether a certain programme or project has accomplished its overall objectives and triggered the desired consequences or some anticipated one or not. This has been the wrong end of the development cycle—too late to affect the social process (Cernea, 1985).

In order that Sociology and Social Anthropology could substantiate their claims for providing operational solutions to the development projects or schemes, there is a need to expand the basic and applied research in both these non-economic disciplines. Over the years, there has been a shift from the traditions of Rural Sociology focusing on rural-urban continuum and diffusion of innovations to Sociology of Agriculture, including farming, animal husbandry, forestry and fishing, crop and farm research systems and irrigation management. Also over the past few decades, peasant studies focusing on the mode of production and social organisations of peasants have provided better insights in understanding the dynamics of the political, social and economic factors in agricultural development among the stratified societies.

Though a large number of anthropologists have been involved in the development oriented research, yet developmental anthropology as an academic subdiscipline has not emerged fully as yet because of lack of coherent conceptual and methodological apparatus. However, developmental anthropology has become an incipient profession and field of study and has produced a body of technically informed, substantive findings on different types of development initiatives, crosscutting the traditional academic and ethnographic categories (Hoben, 1982).

Anthropologists by training develop efficacy in establishing easy rapport with the people. This puts them in an advantageous position to work with the members of the other disciplines in the development projects as well as with communities for whom these development initiatives are made. Some of the broad areas of research by anthropologists and sociologists which could substantiate the development efforts in accomplishing the set goals, are making diagnosis of the community to identify its needs or problems, bridging the gap between real needs and felt needs; social organizations of different groups in the community with a view to understanding the different interaction patterns, stratification and power structure and channels of communication; values, norms and cultural practices of the community which act as barriers or promoters in the change process and finally to locate and identify the leaders for their involvement in the different activities.

Primarily, the focus of sociologists and anthropologists have been to explain or describe past or existing social structures and a very few attempts have been made to look forward and predict change. The disciplines of sociology and social anthropology should not be limited only to analysis and explanation of forces within or outside the system but also to transform the status quo of the system. This would call for suitable methodologies for social action in policy making endeavours, if the role of anthropologists has to become effective in the development milieu (Cernea, 1985).

Planning with people often remains a slogan. The so often talked about people's participation in the development work is an Utopian concept. The community hardly takes upon itself the whole responsibility of development activities and in most cases, people are involved in them whereas their sustained participation remains more of a myth than a reality. Apart from developing suitable sociological methodologies for people's participation, we need to evolve techniques for building grassroot planning, community organizations for farmers, fishermen, women, youth and landless labourers. The scarcity of such sociological and anthropological methodologies reflects the underdevelopment of the applied aspects of these disciplines. There is a need for social scientists to generate new products for use by development practitioners but these should not be regarded as replacing the traditional products of research but as supplementing the methodologies for social action, be they called social technologies, social engineering, socio-techniques, human engineering (Firth, 1981).

Institutionalizing Development Anthropology

In view of the fact that the development milieu over the past few decades is tending to be infrastructural oriented, an anthropologist in the different development initiatives has to be more responsive to it. Basic research may be considered prestigious and the teaching assignment may have an academic glamour for an anthropologist but his or her involvement in the applied field is more challenging. In the recent past, quite a large proportion of the sociologists have moved out of their academic dens and are conscious of the fact that sociological theories have bearing on their planned change. This is also largely due to better awareness of the programme planners and administrators who have started appreciating the relevance of socio-cultural factors in the change process and a need to involve sociologists in the planning and implementation of these programmes.

The alternative perspective on development with its emphasis on "putting people first", would necessitate examining the "full range" of human behaviour, the predictive rather than what people in general do, what things they do most of the time and what they have done up to now. Anthropological theory so far has mainly directed itself towards the latter. Besides, there is a need to look at behavioural frequencies and the alternative procedure and organization that people might take up as they may think necessary in different situations. Although a shift from determinism to a probablistic frame of reference in Social Anthropology became significant by the work of Raymond Firth in the mid-1950s, yet is not fully worked out. In addition to above, there is difficulty of finding people at the right level of ability and using them for a dubious anthropological intervention. These have been observed as two main difficulties in social anthropology in development as a part of an effort to "put people first" (Dyson-Hudson, 1985).

Further ,in order to delineate the role of an anthropologist in the development initiative, one will have to specify the system in which he or she is involved. If the organizational system is the reference point for an anthropologist, then he or she would be in a position to contribute significantly to the development efforts as a member of the development team if predisposed favourably towards other disciplines. It is difficult to be knowledgeable about all the disciplines involved in the development process, but even an understanding and appreciation of other disciplines will go a long way for a sociologist to make him or herself acceptable to the programme planners and administrators.

At the planning and evaluation level, since evaluation is an integral part of the planning process, an anthropologist may help the programme management to identify or locate the factors which may impede the development efforts, and may have to develop an information system from the field upward for more rational decisions of the operations of the programme and to optimize the resources for maximization of outputs. As a part of evaluation efforts, an anthropologist through the feedback and feedforward mechanisms may help in institution building as in the context of the developing nations, it has been observed that the efficiency of an organisation is generally hampered by role diffusedness, structural inconsistency and ad hoc decision making.

However, if the reference point for an anthropologist is the community, then he or she as a member of the planning group of a development project can build data on socio-cultural barriers and promoters of change, identification and location of leaders at the community level and through monitoring and evaluation of programme operations. This may help the management in the accomplishment of the set goals. At the implementation level, an anthropologist may be instrumental in educating and motivating the target groups to adopt some of the desirable practices through diffusion of information by various channels of communication, involving community leadership, voluntary organizations and mobilizing local resources for a wider community participation.

The whole gamut of sociological know-how that can go in making an anthropologist development oriented would necessitate drastic changes in the professional training of sociologists and anthropologists. Unfortunately, the Universities and other academic institutions responsible for the training of sociologists and anthropologists are reacting casually to the preparation of a band of young students in developmental anthropology. The academicians need to become sensitive to this issue and take appropriate measures in instituting necessary changes in the University curricula under the new education policy.

This becomes even more significant in view of thin contents of social sciences in professional technical (engineering), agricultural and medical institutes. Although, it is desirable to integrate sociological know-how into such professional courses, so that technical personnel involved in the development milieu could effectively tackle national or community problems for the accomplishment of set goals, yet it is observed that these technical experts for reasons best known to them, show utter ignorance of the sociological dimensions of technical production processes. There is an urgent need to strengthen social sciences contents of these professional courses. Besides, there is a strong need of involving more and more sociologists and anthropologists into the development projects. This would require sensitization of the administrators and planners of plans, programmes or projects towards such a need.

A mention has earlier been made of the increasing intervention of a social anthropologist and sociologist in social engineering of the development projects. Should or should not an anthropologist act as a practitioner in the development initiatives, this remained as a debatable issue with the anthropologists and sociologists for quite some time. For much of its history, the anthropologists have confined themselves to the traditional role of diagnosticians of the community. However, with development becoming a dynamic concept and with its emphasis on putting people in the centre of the development milieu, an anthropologist would have to increasingly take up his or her role in social policy research analysis or in social engineering so as to transform the fabric of society.

As an Evaluation Sociologist in the Rural Development Project at Mauritius, to begin with my belief has been that an anthropologist or a sociologist should confine him or herself to the diagnosis of the issues so that he or she may not encroach upon the role of other members in the development team. This appeared necessary for institution building in the context of the developing countries with traditional social structures. But as the years passed while I was through the project, let me candidly admit, I started observing a change in my conviction. Limited oneself only to the diagnostic sphere, may restrict the involvement of an anthropologist in the decision-making process as planners and programme administrators may not take cognizance of the factors identified in the diagnosis of the situations or they may pay lipservice to them. In that case, an anthropologist may become an appendix in the organizational setting of the development project.

In the above backdrop, it is imperative for an anthropologist to actively involve him or herself in the implementation of development activities through participation and mobilization of community and be a social engineer in the development process. Social engineering has been defined as an attempt to use body of sociological knowledge in the design of policies or institutions to accomplish some purposes. "Social engineering can be accomplished for a mission oriented agency or for some group opposed to the existing organizational structure or it may be undertaken separately from either. When it is conducted close to the policy making centres, it is often termed social policy analysis, when practised by groups in opposition to current regimes, social engineering becomes social criticism" (Rossi and Whyte, 1983).

However, the efficacy of social engineering in influencing social action will depend upon the creation of suitable methodology or strategy for the development of, for and by people. As intellectuals, we should make an endeavour to develop competence among the anthropologists and sociologists at our universities to influence social action in the different types of development initiatives.

References

Cernea, Michael, (1985), (ed.) *Putting People First: Sociological Variables in Rural Development*, A World Bank Publication, Oxford University Press.

Dyson, Hudson Neville, (1985), "Pastrol Production Systems and Livestock Development Projects: An East African Perspective" in Cernea, Michael (ed.), *Putting People First.* op. cit.

Etzioni, Amital and Eva Etzioni, (1964), *Social Change: Sources, Patterns and Consequences*, New York, Basic Books, Inc. Publishers.

Frank, Andre Gunder, (1983), "Crisis and Transformation of Dependency in the World System" in *Theories of Development* (eds.) Chilcote Ronald H., and Johnson Dale L., Beverly Hills, Sage Publications.

Firth, Raymond, (1981), "Engagement and Detachment: Reflections on Applying Social Anthropology to Social Affairs". *Human*

Organization, Vol. 30, No. 3.

Hoben, Allan, (1982), "Anthropologists and Development" *Annual Review of Anthropology*, Palo Alto.

Mehta, S.R., (1981), *Social Development in Mauritius: A Study of Rural, Modernization in an Island Community*, New Delhi, Wiley Eastern Ltd.

Mehta, S.R., (1984), *Rural Development Policies and Programmes: A Sociological Perspective*, New Delhi, Sage Publications.

Parthasarathy, G., (1982), "Intergrated Rural Development: Concepts, Theoretical Base and Contradiction", in *Development Planning and Policy* (eds.) Gupta, D.B. et.al, New Delhi, Wiley Eastern Limited.

Rogers, Everett M., (1976) (ed.), *Communication and Development*, Beverly Hills, Sage Publications.

Rossi, Peter H., and W.F. Whyte, (1983), "The Applied Side of Sociology", in *Applied Sociology: Roles and Activities of Sociologists in Diverse Settings* (eds.) Freeman H.E. et.al. San Francisco, Jossey-Sass Publishers.

4

Development and Management of Social Tensions

Perspectives on Development

Development has been described as a generic term meaning growth, evolution, stage of inducement or progress (Mehta, 1981). The concept of development gained currency after World War II and has been defined by most economists, in the operational sense, as growth of the per capita GNP or a similar national accounts figure. There has been considerable criticism of this approach to development in view of a large number of developing countries failing to achieve, on an average, a satisfactory rate of growth of per capita GNP. A number of observers have concluded that this has been basically due to the insufficient attention given to social and political factors in planning (Galnoor, 1971).

It has been emphasised that "apart from the 'economic problem' of producing goods and services, we have the 'social problem' of using those resources in such a way as to improve the welfare effect of economic activity" (Drewniwski, 1971). Thus, social indicators have to be considered along with economic indicators of development, as the former reflect the conditions in which people live and this makes the development matrix a complete whole. That is why, of late, it has been started that development is not to be measured in terms of growth only, but is to be explicitly expressed as growth and social change. The element of change has brought along with it the processes of structural differentiation, integration and social disturbances in the institutional set ups for new social order to (Smelser, 1965). Thus qualitative changes must occur concurrently with quantitative changes (Colm and Geiger, 1965).

Development in the new perspective has been referred to as

an overall process of transforming Men and Societies leading to a social order in which every human being can achieve moral and material well being. (FAO) Development has also been referred to as a whole; an integral, value-loaded cultural process encompassing the natural environment, social relations, education, production, consumption and well being (Development Dialogue, 1975).

It is well known that there is really no single theory that could entirely explain the phenomenon of social change. Theories of evolution and revolution have highlighted different aspects of social change but we have yet to find a satisfactory explanation. As such, it may be important to understand the concept of social change. Moore defines it as 'the significant alteration of social structure; that is, of patterns of social action and interaction, including consequences and manifestations of such structures embodying norms, values and cultural products and symbols' (Moore, 1967). He further contends that since there is no singular theory of social structure in more than a differential sense, there is no reason to expect a singular theory of change, since different types of social organisations set different variables for analysing changes in pattern of actions' (Moore, 1965). In the context of planned programmes, we are mainly concerned with planned change or purposeful social change. This has been defined as 'increase in control over the conditions of existence' or alternatively as 'an expansion of resources' (Coleman, 1971). This concept of social change is close to that of social development.

Two paradigms of economic development have been suggested by development planners. (Weaver, 1975) The basic paradigm of traditional economics, based on the concept of 'economic man', stresses the goal of maximum consumption of goods and services with minimum effort. It is assumed that as development proceeds, the capitalist will reinvest and employ more persons, and this will help in the redistribution of income among a larger segment of the population. But this 'grow now' and 'trickle later' approach has failed to tackle the problems of unemployment, inequality of income, regional disparities and the dilemma of poverty, malnutrition and illiteracy fully in the developing nations of the Third World. Currently, they are advocating working for a standard of living consistent with the people's own values. Basic human needs are being stressed over luxury items. Planning for production and distribution should be done simultaneously and the poor should be provided with means so that they can satisfy their needs. Greater emphasis on labour rather than capital-intensive work is being laid to combat the problem of unemployment.

The second paradigm of economic development is historical and holistic, and is advocated by political economists. Their goal of development is based on the liberation of a nation internally as well as from its position of subordination and dependency on highly developed countries. Social ownership, centralised planning to allocate the factors of production (land, labour and capital), and directing the social surplus into productive investments in order to meet people's basic needs are the measures suggested for development. They consider social revolution as a precondition for development.

Perspective on Tension Management System

The equilibrium model of social system does not explain questions pertaining to sources of change. At the best, it predicts one direction of change—change that restores the system to a steady state. Even the Marxist framework advocating destruction in order to establish a new social system for eliminating the dynamic tension generated as a result of interaction of historical dialectical forces is inadequate. The biggest mistake of Marx was that he conceived of an ideal classless society as an ultimate end which in the context of society is somewhat impossible. The main reason is lack of close correspondence between the "ideal" and the "actual" in many contexts of social behaviour of human beings.

Dismissing both these perspectives on social change, Moore, (1965) puts forth his view of society as a tension—management system. According to him, in view of certain amount of flexibilities and uncertainties characteristics of open social systems, tensions, inconsistencies or strains are intrinsic to them. Once these tensions are identified, they can become the probable sites of change. The consequences of change will certainly be tension-producing and also possibly tension-reducing. Further, tension does not mean that change will initially reduce tension. In certain types of sequential analyses, one may identify tension-producing changes rather than change-producing tensions. Finally, the conception of society as a tension management system is not based on the promise that the management is successful or the system persists or it will last long to permit oneself to speak of 'transitions' from one system to another. The probability of these things to happen will be determined by identifying the system and the variables affecting the course of its change; one possible course may be destruction.

In his further analysis, Moore outlines two aspects of the relation between the ideal and actual behaviour that provide universal source of tension and change in social systems. These are, the ubiquity of the "environmental challenge" and the ubiquity of non-conformity and failure to achieve ideal values. Man as a biological creature has to make adjustment in a partially non-human environment and this adjustment may include domination, control or destruction. His actions on "nature" may affect his continued capacity to survive or control without assurance that his efforts will show benign results. Without a total control of human biology and the non-human environment, one can expect ample opportunities for strain and innovation, because "culture" and "setting" are never in perfect adjustment. The second ubiquitous source of change producing strain is due to the inherent fact that social order is a moral order and since "sin" or "non-conformity" occurs in all societies, ideal values are not generally achieved. Further, prescribed behaviour patterns do not remain consistent as roles collide in particular contexts, making ambivalence and ambiguity intrinsic to human condition. The inconsistency between the ideal and the actual is tension-producing and conducive to change. Thus the flexibilities inherent in social systems and the existence of environmental and social challenges respectively provide "chance" variability and selective adaptation and together these enable us to predict cumulative change. In short, in addition to "trivial" changes that do not essentially alter the system and other threatening changes that may either be resisted and suppressed, there is going to be selective adaptation with significant and enduring consequences.

The strain or tension that is predictive of change is mainly between the "part" and the "whole", that is, between the specialized system of action of the "part" and its consequences to the society in which it is located. Within some range, change in certain functions are fulfilled and may make no difference. But beyond that range, changes in the consequences of patterned behaviour will have wider influence both with regard to other patterns and to the way and degree to which the requisites for the survival of society are met.

Another major source of tension in societies, no doubt is inequality but one has to find any one anywhere who truly believes in complete social equality. Moore (1963) argues that "the practice of equal rewards for unequal performance does not immediately recommend itself as either functionally or ethically superior to the contrary scandal of unequal rewards for equal performance". However, the source of inequality as a tension has a potential for change. Eisenstadt also suggests that "conflict" is inherent in any setting of social interaction. He puts forth two main reasons for the same: first, because of the involvement of plurality of actors in any such settings and second, due to the multiplicity of the principles inherent in the institutionalization of any such settings; the multiplicity of institutional principles and of cultural orientations embodying power struggles and conflicts between different groups and movements (Eisenstadt, 1985).

Man's ability to destroy the system by evolving a technology disastrous to mankind and its existence shall have to be discredited. It is in this sense that the conception of Man as a "total making" being shall have to be changed to Man as a "problem solving" entity within a social system. Thus, selective adaptation to social system for responding to the ubiquitous environmental and social institutional changes, perhaps, is the best possible alternative to maintain order of a society than to opt for the destruction of the societal system.

Social Tensions and Unrest

As a result of social and economic differentiation in the villages due to technological innovations (like mechanisation of farms, use of chemical fertilizers, good quality seeds, irrigation facilities such as tubewells, pumps and canals, shifting cropping patterns, double cropping) and farm management measures (like consolidation of landholdings, land tenure reforms and land ceilings, distribution of land to the landless, better price for cash crops and a subsequent interest in marketable produce, fixing of prices by the government for major crops, protests by small and marginal farmers on non-availability or accessibility to farm credit and marketing facilities, agitations for better prices for cash crops, introduction of industrially manufactured goods and the consequent elimination of artisans from the village, exploitation and harassment of lower socio-economic groups by the landowning and money-lending groups, education of the people, migration to cities and migration back to the villages or back to contacts with their families, politicisation of the masses as a consequence of participation in the assembly, parliament and panchayat elections at different levels) have resulted in generating and creating social disturbances and tensions in the villages. Over the years, these tensions have surfaced in view of the inability of institutional frameworks (that is, social, economic and political) to control or integrate these into a new social order. This is mainly because of the vested interests of certain dominant individuals in power, party politics and political instability, diffused and unclear goals of development, international power relations and economic dependency on rich nations.

These social tensions or disturbances are evident in different parts of rural India and have assumed different shapes and forms. There have mainly been agitations by less organised groups, sometimes, protests by effected groups and in rare cases, rebellious violent movements but all these tendencies have been spread sporadically over different regions, and have been limited in intensity and controlled by the manipulative mechanism of the State machinery. In villages, social tensions are often due to class interests, conflicts between Scheduled Castes and non-Scheduled Castes or between landless labourers and landowning group farmers' agitations for better prices and communal feelings and religion. These social tensions have led to separatist tendencies and impede the development process both in the urban and rural areas. Further, there is a clash of interests between the urban and rural elites who are apparently in league with the State machinery as many of them directly or indirectly support and represent the State. Politicisation of the masses and the non-availability of avenues for leadership because of the reluctance of those in power to surrender it, the lack of clear vision and commitment of leaders at all levels and the inability of the State to integrate social organisations and values, are some of the main reasons which, if not contained or controlled by the State, will lead to social movements, necessitating a new social order.

Changes in Agrarian and Social Relationships

The developmental inputs during the past few decades have yielded certain outputs but the effects of these have not been what were intended. Economic development remained dictated by the political elites who, in order to maintain their positions, exploited people along commercial, regional and linguistic lines. There has been an increase in the separatist tendencies within states as well as between states, besides the concentration of wealth with a small segment of the population and a rise in black money resulting in a parallel economy. Political life has been an overriding factor over economic life and these together, in an undesired mix, have resulted in the fast deterioration of standards in public life or moral values and the cultural ethos upheld in Indian society. These and various other external factors (including the influence of market economies of the developed world, the oil and energy crisis and world inflationary trends at global level, and nuclear rivalries of the big powers) have created tensions and the villages cannot escape the negative impact of these factors. The village community is shorn today more than it was ever before. The isolable, self-contained and self-sufficient village community is a past story. Certain significant changes are reported in the agrarian relations in the village which have consequently affected the social relationships between different social and economic groups.

M. Zaheer has highlighted two factors which may have been responsible for bringing about changes in agrarian relations in some parts of the country (Zaheer, 1975). One is technological advancement in agriculture and the second is related to the politicisation of agricultural labourers. The first has brought about changes in the landlord-tenant relations while the latter has affected cultivator relations.

However, Alexander, after briefly mentioning the Ministry

of Home Affairs Report (1969) on the subject presented two schools of thought who view the changes in agrarian relations as being due to two different sets of factors (Alexander, 1980).

One view is that the increase in agricultural production marked as a result of breakthroughs in high-yielding varieties of seeds and other agricultural practices associated with new technology. The large and medium level-farmers who could afford these inputs raised their income levels considerably whereas the small cultivators and landless labourers were left far behind. This created an economic hiatus between the rich and the poor cultivators in the villages and agrarian unrest became manifest. The second view is that the introduction of new values envisaging greater egalitarian relations in various aspects of social life due to legislative and economic measures for the weaker sections of society made the concerned people conscious of the various aspects of social life as exploitative. It is this perception of the situation which may have created a feeling of dissatisfaction about the existing labourer-cultivator relationship among a section of the labourers. Thus, the changing values and norms of society have been responsible for agrarian unrest.

In his study on agrarian tensions in Thangarpur (Tamil Nadu), Alexander (1981) reported that 'agrarian unrest was a manifestation of the conflict arising out of the endeavours of the weaker sections of society to enhance their status and benefits and the endeavours made by the privileged sections to prevent it'. But this unrest helped the labourers to enhance their status and equalitarian social relations emerged. However, his study on the social development of weaker sections in Andhra Pradesh shows that Harijans interacted with higher castes in various public places but their relations in private were limited (Alexander, 1981). Despite their overcoming many of the traditional bonds and the observance of untouchability, they have yet to be accepted as social equals by higher castes.

Apart from these economic and cultural factors there are other factors which are also responsible for agrarian unrest. Social mobility, especially among the lower castes, due to greater educational and occupational opportunities; migration to towns and cities for better jobs, movement of labourers to the Gulf countries resulting in heavy remittances to their homeland, and the politicisation of labourers in terms of their power to vote, have also helped to create tensions and unrest between different social and economic groups.

Although the situation is not as bad as it used to be about five decades ago, yet the exploitation of the weaker sections by the higher castes and higher income groups still prevails to a large extent. The landless, and especially the Harijans have for centuries, occupied the lowest position in the social stratification system in the villages and the acceptance of this fact has led them to believe that this state of affairs is ordained by God because of their past karma and they have to suffer because they are destined to do so as members of the 'community of fate'. This has a dampening effect on their organisation and they tend to develop apathy, indifference and a lethargic attitude. This is further augmented by the fact of marginality, as the poverty group tends to get perpetuated from one generation to the other. Unless these people are helped by some outside agencies, political or social, and shaken out of the 'culture of poverty', this group has little chance of acquiring equality. The factor of caste hierarchy in India makes Marxism a difficult proposition. Even a state like West Bengal (which has used party cadres in panchayat and assembly elections), has a majority of persons belonging to the higher caste groups. Whether caste can cross economic barriers and become a class is yet to be substantiated on a wider scale for providing a perspective. One may have individual instances of a Harijan acquiring presidentship of a village panchayat or samiti or becoming members of Parliament or legislatures, or putting up business, and commercial enterprises but Harijans, as a group, have remained where they were in real economic and social terms. However, the situation is changing and has changed. Help to the Harijans from outside agencies, extension networks, voluntary organisations (like Agency of Voluntary Organisation for Rural Development) have made inroads in certain areas on a limited basis to break the caste and kinship ties of the higher caste groups and develop lowercast groups on cooperative lines in trades like tannery and leather work, weaving and other crafts. In an interesting article, Mathai (Mathai, 1980) narrates the story of Lumbaram whose position in the economic and social system of the village was fixed as a *raiger* (a shoemaker) and who sat with his eyes lowered, silent and a coward while a volley of questions were being shot by the land owing *Ravat* Sarpanch. He shows how the 'Lumbarams' of India need to know the skills of managing their affairs and 'not be entirely submerged by the management of the system that engulfs them'. In the process of self-reliance, Lumba and his associates or group have to establish a free flow of information, get united to withstand repercussions, and demand the accountability of the administrators and the politicians. They have to choose whether to remain captive or not, and make efforts for them or others who want to move from economic and political captivity towards freedom. Although Lumba has gained confidence and can take decisions for himself as well as for his group, yet he has a long way to attain the road to self-reliance. If such 'Lumbas' multiply on our vast land quicker and faster, then there could be some hope of change or at least bringing about change in the present system of power. This anecdotal but analytical story has brought into focus the need to organise the rural poor who are rather weak. It is only the political parties that can organise them as the government cannot do so.

But on the other hand, the privileged groups in the villages, farmers and cultivators, are getting organised. The Akhil Bhartiya Kisan Sangh (All India Kisan Union) has been formed to ask for better prices for crops from the government. Sharad Pawar, leader of the Shetkari Sanstha, gave a lead march to the growers and they asked for more money for their onion crop in Maharashtra. Better prices are also being asked for wheat, rice and sugarcane.

The social fabric of village life has not been devoid of tensions either. Economic gains within a family created individual jealousies and even socio-economic jealousies became visible between different families in the villages due to the demonstration effects of consumer goods and electrical gadgets. The claim on land, as provided by law, is also being demanded by daughters in the family along with sons. This has also resulted in creating enormous tensions. Sham Lal, dismissing the pseudo-radical approach of intellectuals whose work is long in theory and short in practice, concludes that:

> The tensions which are developing in rural society can be an incentive to overdue changes in the balance of power and a

faster pace of progress only if they are managed with great skill and not allowed to get beyond the point of no return. Beyond this point they can only disrupt the process of development and further slow it down, with terrible consequences not only for rural society but for the country as a whole (Shamlal 1981).

This caution needs to be taken by the national leadership in the good spirit and perspective and tension-management mechanisms have to be evolved which should be pragmatic to reduce situations creating tensions.

Management of Social Tensions

The management of social tensions in the villages, which have been mounting over the years as a consequence of increasing disparities between different social and economic groups have to be kept at a minimum level. It is impossible to completely eliminate conflicts in society. Some of these are unavoidable and may be counter-productive or productive to the system.

The source of power lies in the social system. The aim of the democratic development process is to redistribute wealth, power and status but the government's programmes do not concentrate on this. There is a need to involve committed people outside the political and administrative set-up (such as academicians, doctors and engineers) who should intervene in the planning and implementation of government policies and plans. They, along with voluntary organisations engaged in rural development, should help organise the poor in the villages.

The people in the villages are very patient. They accept the concepts of *karma* and *dharma* without questioning why the more affluent are getting the major benefits of the development process. Fast urban development is further depriving them. There is a polarisation of the two worlds of the poor and the rich. We should ensure that the poor do not become more poor. If rural drudgery continues, it will drive the rural poor out of the villages. This will lead to the creation of slums in the cities. Clashes between the landless labourers and prosperous farmers can be managed by the organization of the poor by committed people and those concerned about distributive justice. The landless labourers are not so particular about owning land but better wages for their hard work is what matters most to them. This can scale down the profit of the landlords considerably.

Rural youth in this poverty groups should be identified. Through `non-political movements' and the `social consciousness approach' they should be organised on economic issues that concern and confront them. They can become a political force in the social system and provide a constructive framework for distributive justice. The rural poor must get a relatively better share if conflicts and social tensions are to be minimised. Making them self-reliant by providing them with the necessary knowledge and skills so that they can liberate themselves from economic and social exploitation should be the main focus of rural development.

Development planning and political ideology are mutually inclusive. Whereas communists propogate the use of compulsion, coercion or force to influence individuals and groups for decision-making, capitalists employ the power of the media to influence decisions. Compulsion, force or suppression is not applicable in our situation. The caste system is peculiar to India and religious values do not allow suppression. Moreover, change associated with education is more self-sustained and we should not attempt to bring in change by compulsion. Instead, change should be brought about by informing others and discussing it with them so that it is socially acceptable. However, the control of capitalists on communication through mass media should be checked and the State should evolve a suitable communication policy and strategy to solve developmental problems related to social tensions (Mehta, 1984).

References

Alexander, K.C., (1980), "Economic Development and Social Change", *Behavioural Sciences and Rural Development*. 3, 2 (July), Hyderabad, NIRD

Alexander, K.C., et al., (1981), "Social Development of Weaker Sections in Krishna District", *Behavioural Sciences and Rural Development*. 4, 2 (July), Hyderabad, NIRD

Changing Agrarian Relations in India, (1975) papers and proceedings of a

Seminar held at NICD (5-6 April 1971), Hyderabad National Institute of Community Development.

Coleman, James S., (1971), "Conflicting Theories of Social Change", *American Behavioural Scientist*, 14, 5, (May/June).

Colm, Gerhard and Geiger Theodore, (1965), 'Country Programming as a Guide to Development', in Robert E. Asher et, al. (eds.), *Development of Emerging Countries: An Agenda for Research*, Washington, D.C., Brokings Institution, p. 47.

Drewniwski, Jan, 1971, "The Practical Significance of Social Information", *Annals of the American Academy of Political and Social Science*, (January), p. 84.

Eisenstadt, S.N., (1985), "Macro-Societal Analysis-background, development and Indications" in *Macro-Sociological Theory*, Volume 1 (eds.) S.N. Eisenstadt and H.J. Helle, Beverly Hills, Sage Publications.

Food and Agriculture Organisation (FAO), United Nations Rome, *Study Guide on Development*, Freedom from Hunger Campaign/Action for Development, p. 5.

Galnoor, Itzhak, (1971), "Social Information for What", *The Annals of the American Academy of Political and Social Science*, January, p. 8.

Lal, Sham, (1981), "The Changing Village: (I) The Geography of Hunger; (II) Unstable Equilibrium; (III) Tensions and Challenges", *The Times of India*, 29, 30 June and 1 July 1981.

Mathai, Ravi J., (1980), "Investing in Democracy (II)-Captivity or Self-Reliance", *Mainstream*, (20 December).

Mehta, S.R., (1981), *Social Development in Mauritius: A Study on Rural Modernization of an Island Community*, New Delhi, Wiley Eastern, p. 1.

Mehta, S.R., (1984), *Rural Development Policies and Programmes:* A *Sociological Perspective*, New Delhi, Sage Publications.

Moore, Wilbert E., (1963), "But some are more equal than others", American Sociological Review, pp. 13-18.

Moore, Wilbert E., (1965), *Social Change*, New Delhi, Prentice-Hall of India.

Moore, Wilbert E., (1967), *Order and Change*, New York, John Wiley & Sons, p. 3.

Smelser, Neil, J., (1965), *The Sociology of Economic Life*, New Delhi, Prentice Hall of India.

The 1975 Dag Hammarskjold Report on Development and International Cooperation, 'Introduction—To Set in Motion the Process of Change', *Development Dialogue*, 1/2, 1975, p. 7.

Weaver, James H., (1975), 'Economic Development: Two Paradigms', *Development Studies Programme*, Washington, D.C., Agency for International Development, Transcript of a talk.

6

Development in India: Structural-Functional Perspective

Continuity and change in and of the different forms of societies at various points of time has been and is still the prime concern of sociologists. The ideas thrown up by the founding fathers—Comte, Spencer, Durkheim, Marx and Weber have been pursued by the contemporary sociologists and attempts have been made by some to provide comprehensive insights and understanding of various human groups and larger social configurations from different perspectives and point of views.

Broadly, we can conceive two dominant paradigms of development within evolutionary and revolutionary perspectives of sociology, that is, structural-functional and conflict or dialectical with certain elements of interpretative sociology built in them.

In the evolutionary or structural-functional perspective of development, the emphasis is on movement from a less to a more differentiated social form through processes of ever more complex specialization and functional interdependence. As society develops, certain 'adaptive features' are incorporated which increase the capacity of the system to adapt to its environment. Such a view of development is observed in the themes on modernization. In short, the development of traditional societies in modern ones is, thus, a contemporary intellectual extension of social Darwinian evolution (Rogers, 1976).

On the other hand, in conflict or dialectical perspective of development, the basic course of development is the internal contradictions within a society, that is between forces of production and relations of production resulting in contradictions between classes and between the old and the new structures. These contradictions push the society towards a new and better social order. It is argued that the development of a nation is possible only if it can free itself both externally and internally from its dependency on the capitalist system. But in a pessimistic note, Frank expresses that the socialist countries which should have moved from socialism to communism are getting back to capitalist economic system (Frank, 1983).

Both these perspectives of development have been criticised for their logical imperfections as well as for their empirical distortions, apart from their ideological predilections. However, in the context of a developing nation, it is the aspirations and preparation of people which should be the main cause and consequence of economic and social development (Mehta, 1987).

We have now the conception of 'Another Development', which emphasizes that people of the Third World nations must strive to be more self-reliant and cooperative. They should get together, plan and share responsibility for the affairs of their community. Besides, they should cooperate and share the goods and services produced relevant to their needs and with resources available in or around them to enhance the quality of life for most of the people than for a pampered few. This would necessitate doing without most of the luxuries, fashionable clothes, possessions of gadgets and looking forward to a more comfortable and convenient lifestyle within one's means and in consistent with one's values. Thus, 'Another Development' calls for frugal, self-reliant and cooperative approach. A real transformation of people leading to development would mean satisfaction of basic human needs under humane and equitable conditions. This would necessitate a deep serious concern to understand the world as a unity (Moshoeshoe, II, 1987).

Some of the ideas contained above are based on the remark of Mahatma Gandhi, "there is sufficiency in the world for Man's needs; but there is not enough for Man's greed". Gandhian philosophy of Man in relation to Society focuses on satisfaction of basic human needs rather than greed and treating work not as a disutility but as a fulfilment of personality. Further, Gandhi emphasized on decentralization of government and on a technology which serves social needs. These ideas are significant for the development of the Third World countries. Even Gunnar

Myrdal, in his *Asian Drama* emphasized on institutions and attitudes in the development of the Third World countries. These have to be considered not in isolation but in their mutual relationship for the development purposes. Further, the identification of target areas and target groups has not only helped the intended beneficiaries of the developmental inputs but it has also highlighted the concept of 'Putting People First' in the development milieu (Cernea, 1985). Some of these ideas helped me in developing a perspective on rural development in our context.

An expanded concept of development has brought in development initiatives from various perspectives (Structural-Functional, Conflict, Gandhian, Voluntaristic, Ethnic, etc.) and one has to visualize the development efforts in a society from personality, social, economic, cultural and political dimensions. This would demand two types of commitments from the sociologists. First, in view of a large canvas to be covered in development and inadequacy of a particular sociological perspective to comprehend it in totality, various social and psychological perspectives connected with human action shall have to be considered and different aspects of development to be explained differently with separate long and short range perspectives (Mehta, 1984). Secondly, the sociologists should not confine themselves only to analysis and explanation of forces within or outside the social system but also to transform the status quo of the system. This would call for suitable methodologies of social action in policy making endeavours, if the role of sociologists has to become effective in the development initiatives (Cernea, 1985; Firth, 1981).

Structural-Functional Perspective and Development: A Case of Rural Development in India

In the Indian context, the conflict perspective of development within the Marxian stream of thought and as advocated by political economists, has hardly a place in the development of our nation because of socio-political and cultural considerations which are not conducive for a revolutionary change. As such, one has to conceive of development initiatives in India within a structural-functional perspective of development (The other perspectives of development such as

Gandhian, Voluntaristic or Ethnic, are mainly derivatives of the above).

To start with, I may like to examine the relevance of the revolutionary approach to development for rural areas in our country. Based mainly on Chinese experiment for mass participation and committed leadership, this strategy of rural development was proletariat oriented, collectivity sanctioned and involved grassroots planning and leadership. The policies of development thus evolved were carried out by disciplined and indoctrinated party cadres under strict party and government control. Under the broad political system and liberal ideology in India, it is impossible to adopt such a coercive method. The Indian tradition is characterized by a cultural ethos and value system embedded in our religious philosophy and Hindu way of life.

Some of the major values upheld in our society are conciliation or reconciliation, tolerance, sympathy, hierarchy, affection and warmth expressed through sentiments and emotions, belief in an Almighty God as a creator, preserver and destroyer of the universe, fructification of actions according to one's Karma or deeds, spirituality and belief in reincarnation, mutual help or cooperation, hospitality and concern for the needy and suffering lots. Although modernising influences have affected some of these values, yet preference is given to these over values of conflict, intolerance, hostility, rudeness, rationality and reward according to one's efforts, self-orientation and materialism.

Note that these values are non-existent in Indian society but traditional values are still strongly upheld by a large segment of the population. Moreover, socio-structural aspects like caste and kinship networks still persist and play a dominant role in establishing connubial relationships. Economic development and the politicization process along with legal measures taken by the State, have not been effective in breaking up social solidarities such as caste and kinship. Electoral alliances are formed around these groups and caste still reckons as an important factor in Indian politics.

Further, if we look back at the political incidents in the pre-Independence era which led to the freedom of the country, we find that practically all violent, rebellious and revolutionary moves made by Indians against the Britishers for freedom proved abortive or unsuccessful. Instead, the silent march, the satyagrah movement, civil disobedience, fast unto death, dogged persistence, perseverance and self-control as a means of securing freedom were followed4 by national leaders. This long and continued non-violent struggle for freedom has been embedded and ingrained into the value system of Indian society.

In the above backdrop, it may sound difficult to institute changes or adopt methods of development through coercion and use of force as these may appear counter-productive to a social order which has adopted reconciliation rather than conflict as a process of continuity.

One may, however, argue that due to increasing disparities in income during the last five decades of planning, there have been from time to time rising social tensions, rebellious and violent movements, social unrest and agitations in different parts of the country, sporadically. These tensions might be considered preludes to a revolutionary movement subsequently but they can be maintained within a democratic framework and through the revitalization of an institutional framework for efficient production and fair distribution. The political maturity which India has shown during the last five decades as a democratic nation in terms of accepting or rejecting people's representatives according to their roles rather than to their charisma, indicates that given the political will, commitment, and democratic ideals should not belie our expectations. Assuming that there is no possibility of revolution in the country during this century, pragmatically, one can visualize rural development within the evolutionary or structural-functional perspective (Mehta, 1984). In a study done by me on rural development mainly through discussion held with key informants and observations made in field situations, development has been conceived as an overall process of transforming Men and Societies to a social order in which every human being may be able to achieve moral and material well-being consistent with one's values and traditions.

In the light of the above analysis, I have argued that economic development cannot take place without a change in the value system and social organisation of the people in our villages. On the basis of thorough diagnosis of the problems, issues, difficulties confronted in the development of rural areas, certain institutional, technological, infrastructural, participative and human development service-oriented changes have been suggested to affect the village social structure in terms of occupational diversification, social mobility, reduction in income disparities and changes in values and social relationships for an integrated social living. These changes can be effected through decentralized planning and the consequent involvement and commitment of community leaders for implementation of the plans and programmes at district level and below (Mehta, 1984).

Specifically, to tackle the major problem of rural poverty a target group approach has to be followed and one can identify three main groups of landless labourers, women and youth (14-24 years including girls) among the weaker sections of the village community. These target groups should be approached through decentralization of politico-economic activities, encouraging their greater participation in identifying the local resources and matching these with economic activities suitable to their needs and requirements.

Participation of such people in development initiatives will help them to have greater commitment to action and in generating self-reliance necessary for shedding dependency. Institutional changes in land structure, panchayati raj system and cooperative movement need to be done simultaneously in order to make participation process a reality. Instead of implanting economic activities on rural poor, they should be involved to identify the type of activities they would like to pursue and necessary means may be provided to them to undertake these.

Appropriate technology suitable to local needs or requirements has to be invented so that it is economically viable, technically feasible and socially acceptable to the villagers. Industrialization process will have to be hastened and industries especially agro-based such as sugar, cotton-ginning, oil seeds, etc., be brought as early and close to rural areas so as to promote occupational diversification. A geophysical and social analysis of the areas and nature of industries to be introduced will have to be done by the planners and administrators before these are brought to the rural areas. The industries thus established in rural areas can have skill development programmes for the rural labour force unabsorbed by the agricultural sectors so as to initiate the occupational diversification process. This occupational diversification in due course of time, will break up the caste and kinship solidarities by delinking traditional occupations with castes in our villages and consequently affecting the social class and the opinions, attitudes, values and value-orientations of people embedded in our social structure.

No doubt, infrastructural development, self-employment schemes, cooperative efforts for landless women and youth will generate greater employment and wage earning opportunities, thus, raising the purchasing power of the villagers, but all these development initiatives will not make any dent without human, social-service oriented development changes in education, health and population control. Education should help the poor to acquire appropriate knowledge and skills for productive work and overcome dogmatism. Positive health is equally a necessary condition to make them productive on jobs. A check on population growth is equally essential for sustained development. It is also suggested that national leadership should show up commitment and pursue rural development as a policy requiring top priority and attention rather than treating it in a piecemeal fashion as an appendix to the Five-Year Plans.

The national policy on rural development, thus conceived should be followed through a suitable organisational structure from national through state to district level; autonomous in form and based on the principle of 'Putting People First' in the development initiatives (Mehta, 1984). In addition, there is a need to cut on consumer demands and to encourage frugality among the people. If the national leadership fails to pursue these programmes and policies, there would be risks of running in for negative develoment, false modernization effects and irrational attitudes (Mehta, 1981).

The paradigm on Rural Development, with a focus on institutional, technological, infrastructural, participative and social service-oriented changes, may appear rehashing of the old elements of the rural social system but it provides several 'adaptive and integrative features' to maintain and perpetuate a social order in our society within the structural-functional perspective.

Developmental Issues of Sociological Import

If we have to examine some of the developmental issues which have sociological import from the point of view of structural-functional perspective, then we may have to analyse some of the main differentiation processes, integrative mechanisms and the intended or unintended consequences resulting in certain social disturbances in our social system. My study on rural development shows that social and economic differentiation in the villages due to technological innovations (like mechanization of farms, use of chemical fertilizers, good quality seeds, shifting cropping patterns, double cropping patterns and farm management measures like consolidation of land holdings, land tenure reforms and land ceiling, distribution of land to the landless and better prices for cash crops, introduction of industrially manufactured goods and the consequent elimination of artisans from the village, exploitation and harassment of lower socio-economic groups by the land-owning and money lending groups, education of the people, migration to cities and migration back to the villages or back contacts with families, politicization of the masses as a consequence of participation in the assembly, parliament and panchayat elections at different levels), have resulted in generating and creating social disturbances and tensions in the villages. Over the years, these have become more visible in view of inability of institutional framework, i.e., social, economic and political to integrate these into a new social order. This is mainly because of the vested interests of certain dominant individuals in power, party politics and political instability, diffused and unclear goals of development, centralized development planning, international power relations and economic dependency on rich nations (Mehta, 1984).

While making analysis of Rural Development, it is also observed that despite stupendous achievements made in agricultural production and infrastructural systems in the villages, and improving the educational and health status of the villagers, rural poverty is still very extensive and there is a widening of disparities between social and economic groups.

In short the development process has been observed to be

lopsided. The urban areas have grown at the cost of rural areas. This may be primarily because of the continued emphasis by the government in developmental inputs in urban areas, recurring input/output costs in urban areas on the assets created, the higher growth of population in rural areas, the transfer of rural money to urban areas and persisting inflation. Besides, there is a strong lobby of certain pressure groups on the governing States and in view of their vested interests, policies and plans get distorted and mutilated to suit their needs and requirements. (These pressure groups are mainly represented by large-scale industrial units, wholesale traders, rich peasants or rural elites, trade unions of industrial workers and unions of organized sectors).

As a consequence of the socio-economic and political differentiation processes set in and due to lack of adequate integrative mechanisms, the main problems confronted in regard to the development of rural areas have been the shifting focus on the components of rural development rendering institutional structures inadequate and non-viable; increasing disparities between rural and urban areas and within different social groups; ineffectiveness of land reform measures, limited land availability, failure of rural cooperatives; inadequate development of agro-based and other allied industries, defunct Panchayati Raj institutions adversely affecting the participation of the people in the decision-making process, insufficient involvement of youth and women in rural cooperatives and other development activities, skewed distribution of social services such as education and health, increasing pressure of population, inadequate communication facilities, increasing migration of youth to urban centres; and increasing social tensions in the villages (Mehta, 1984).

It is just possible that the antecedents to development were not adequately taken into account while exercising development planning. Our development plans lacked direction and clarity of goals. Besides, they may not be related to the value framework and social organizational aspects of our people. Also, at the implementation level, there is lack of commitment of people at the helm of affairs. As such, due to inadequate 'people's component' in development planning, organizational inefficiency and lack of political will to get plans and schemes implemented at various levels, there is a need to examine whether decentralized planning could be an alternative in the development planning of a country of continental size such as ours within the democratic ideal and structural-functional approach. One may raise the issue if centralized planning has failed, what is the guarantee that the decentralized planning will work? One may argue that it is only through the participation of people in development activities that one can ensure their commitment to develop themselves as well as their community and to build up confidence in them to take decisions on their own and be self-reliant.

Another developmental issue of sociological import is that rural development cannot be conceived in isolation. It is to be considered as an integral part of the total social and economic development of a nation. Economic development has taken precedence over social development and this structural inconsistency often results in cultural lag and the two development processes become incompatible with each other. In fact, all economic phenomena are social phenomenan and together these constitute a social reality. The interrelatedness of these two sets of factors demands an integrated approach to development planning in the rural areas. However, we have yet to come across an approach to rural development which is integrated in content and action for the upliftment of our people. Besides, an interface between rural and urban areas is to be considered while planning rural development activities as urban centres constitute the immediate environment for adaptation purposes.

Land is a limiting factor and to hasten the development of rural areas, there is an urgent need to bring in industries as close and as early to them, with a view to affecting occupational diversity and break caste and kinship solidarities. This is significant from the sociological point of view, so far as development is concerned.

The inadequacy observed in regards to institutional arrangements established at the local level as well as at the higher echelons either through new institution building efforts or modifications of the existing ones, reflected weak integrative mechanisms required to stabilize the differentiation processes set in by various development initiatives. Apart from the problems of organizational and leadership structures, the normative or legal aspect of institutions such as related to activities of land reforms, cooperatives and village councils (Panchayati Raj System) need strengthening, especially at the stage of implementation of the activities. Thus, institution building at local level is another significant developmental issue from the sociological point of view.

Further, my study points out that the conception of development is to be centred around 'people' who are the targets as well as the resources for development. The potential of tapping the huge human resource through appropriate technological, educational and health inputs, is significant for rural development.

To make the various 'adaptive and integrative features' functional within the structural-functional perspective of development, political will of national leadership, perhaps, is the single most imperative or prerequisite for development. This is what is lacking and this needs to be generated to make development a reality in our setting.

References

Cernea, Michael, (ed.), (1985), *Putting People First : Sociological Variables in Rural Development*, A World Bank Publication, Oxford University Press.

Firth, Raymond, (1981), *Engagement and Detachment : Reflections on Applying Social Anthropology to Social Affairs, Human Organization, Vol. 30, No. 3.*

Frank, Andre Gunder, (1983), *Crisis and Transformation of Dependency in the World System*, Chilcote, Ronald H. and Johnson, Dale L. (eds.), *Theories of Development, Beverly Hills, Sage Publications.*

Mehta, S.R., (1981), *Social Development in Mauritius : A Study on Rural Modernization in an Island Community*, New Delhi, Wiley Eastern Ltd.

Mehta, S.R., (1984), *Rural Development, Policies and Programmes: A Sociological Perspectives*, New Delhi, Sage Publications.

Mehta, S.R., (1987), *Communication and Development: Concepts and Methods, Sociological Bulletin,* Vol. 36, No. 1, March.

Moshoeshoe II, (1987), *Alternative Strategies for Development : A Clarion Call, Development Dialogue, No. 1.*

Rogers, Everett M. (ed.), (1976), *Communication and Development,* Beverly Hills, Sage Publications.

7

Globalization, Ethnicity and Development: A Value Perspective

This article contains five parts. In the first portion, an attempt has been made to throw light on the globalization process as well as on the conception of globalization with a view to highlight some of the emerging trends on the world scene. The second part deals with the formation of ethnic identities in reaction to the globalization process and in response to cultural sensitivity. While the third section views global solidarity in terms of one world or several, the fourth part highlights the issues of global development whereas the fifth section proposes a value perspective on global development.

Globalization: Process, Concept and Emerging Trends

Globalization as a process dates back to the discovery of America by Columbus but as a concept, it got currency during the post war era. Colonization across nations was also an accelerating factor towards its promotion. International trade, migration and military interventions further accentuated the globalization process. But, it is during the last five decades or so, due to the information revolution through the affluence of knowledge, satellite and telecommunication networks and fax and video technology that the concept of global "village" has been evolved.

The modernization theorists who treated industrialization as synonymous with development visualized greater homogenization of the world through shared value patterns. As such, global citizenship, civil society, international cooperation and economic order, transnational economy, equity and distributive justice, human consideration and social integration, unipolar political power structure and cultural cooperation became the lofty ideals for the world development. However, the evidence during the last decade or so suggests that instead of homogenizing the world social order, there is a greater heterogeneity than expected as a consequences of developmental initiatives (Mehta, 1992). This warrants examining the concept of globalization and the developmental initiatives.

The main difficulty in comprehending global problems is that globalization is often viewed as homogenization since global phenomena are defined as those that affect all human beings on this planet. Theoretically speaking, this may be true but in reality, at the empirical level, neither the causes of global problems nor the consequences of them have been observed to be homogeneous. Instead, they are heterogeneous and any kind of perceptions and understanding about them will also be heterogeneous as they are mostly based on group interests or local, that is, national settings. It is argued that there is a need to conceive the term "global" in the sense of viewing such problems as "universal" and demanding equal responsibility of all nations and social groups to tackle them in a form acceptable to both the developed and the developing world (Arizpe, 1992).

The homogenization power of mass media having magic multiplying effects on the behaviour patterns of people, also belied the expectation of the modernization theorists as in Europe alone, there are more than 3000 languages spoken. Besides, in the international sphere, where cultural cooperation is vouched for a "global" village concept, it is cultural conquest rather than cooperation which appears to be visible on the world scene (For example, when Macdonald started selling Hamburgers in Russia, the Media bombardment was, 'we would Macdonaldize Russia'. Even, when the *Playboy* magazine was, initiated in Hungary, the Media slogan was that 'we would change the sexual behaviour of the people') (Hamelink, 1990).

After the failure of the homogenization process of the modernists, the second generation development theorists influenced by the dependency theory raised a voice against the expansion of multinational corporations. Their hope of giving power to the States through people's revolution was dashed to ground because of a strong hold of the international capitalist economic order. The breaking up of the socialist world has further demolished the image of the political economy perspective of development. Ethnodevelopment through people's movements and organizations and based on popular culture, appear to be an alternative perspective attractive to some group of theorists for an authentic and genuine development.

Of late, some development theorists have emphasized on a communication model of development based on the formation of a common national culture, fostering political, economic and socio-cultural negotiation. Mass media in this process of development may play a significant role in negotiating cultural conflicts and agreeing on common roles (Servaes, 1986). This perspective has relevance for developmental initiatives at the "global" level through negotiation of certain issues having universal attention and action based on shared values through integrative institutional apparatus.

Keeping the above perspectives in view, one may like to highlight the emerging trends in the world scenario. A succinct review of today's world may point to the dismantling of the East-West divide, end of cold war and erosion of superpower rivalries and to the emergence of a "new world order" based on cooperation rather than on antagonism. Further, there has been sustained economic growth in the west during the post-war period and lesser threat to the world financial markets due to decreased international debt crisis. Moreover, some of the poor countries have been supporting the effective uses of the development strategies of the rich countries. Again, the decade of 1980s which was predicted as a disaster decade for them, did not turn out to be so. However, for the developing world, the decade of 1980s was a period of stagnation and contraction rather than of sustained growth. Debt burden, net transfer of resources from developing to the developed world, low commodity prices and international monetary disorder not only brought disaster to these nations but pushed nearly one billion to live in absolute poverty. Their living standards are lower than what they were thirty years ago. Further, there is a greater intensification of their struggle for existence with a few prospects for improvement. Besides, new issues of global concern such as the state of the environment and the disruption of the ecological systems, the rise of nationalism, growth in the number of "economic" refugees, increase in racial and ethnic conflicts; erosion in the exercise of powers of the National State, increasing role of the non-State actors in international financial and economic relations, continued growth of expenditure on armaments, weapons of mass distruction and on sophisticated weapon systems despite the end of cold war have come to the forefront. It is stated that the world of 1990s and onwards will witness greater complexity of issues and greater interdependence since it may be difficult to tackle problems, in isolation from one another. Poverty, population growth, underconsumption for many and overconsumption for a few, economic and political security problems and greater inequality in between and within nations will be on the rise. Besides, there will be a less clear hierarchy of issues and of purposes than it is today (Claus, 1991).

A synoptic view of the emerging trends at the global level (divided into North and South or the developed and the developing world) sends pessimistic signals about initiatives for global development.

Ethnic Identities: In Response to Globalization Process and Cultural Sensitivity

Some believed that ethnicity was a stage of socio-political evolution preceding the modern, democratic institutions. This had led to consider the developing countries of South as bound by ethnicity. On the other side, the developed countries of North had evolved democratic systems that had taken care of "ethnic" or regional groups and provided political stability. However, in the present set up, it is observed that the above proposition is wrong as ethnicity seems to have surfaced in almost all political systems, not only in the developing but also in the developed world. As anthropologists have been suggesting, ethnicity should not be viewed in the above context, instead it should be taken to mean as the "inherent capacity of any human society to create symbolic, linguistic and social codes to bind its members together". In other words, ethnicity should represent a system of codes that gives meaning, identity and a sense of belonging, thereby, creating boundaries that distinguish one group from the other. A distinction has also been suggested between ethnicity and ethnicism as ethnicism involves "deliberate use of ethnic symbols and codes of conduct to rally round" with a view to defend one's group or attack others in order to accomplish the perceived goals of the group. These ethnic allegiances or identities became more marked after sixties as job and employment opportunities shrunk even in the Western Europe and in the United States of America despite these having the longest period of sustained economic growth and affluence. There, the "comparative advantage" in jobs got started being viewed as "ethnic" advantage of one dominant group over the other (Arizpe, 1992). The situation in the developing countries was still worse as the unemployment rolled on manyfolds in them, due to tough competition in the limited job market.

Despite a halting process in the social mobility of individuals and groups not only in the developed but in the developing world, modernization theorists and even the other development paradigms, have been raising hopes and aspirations of the people towards better quality of life and improvements in their living standards. The homogenisation process of the globe boomeranged the development paradigms and marginalized a large number of groups from the benefits of development. This became much more pronounced in the developing world where a small section of the population was beneficiary of the high technology and industrialized economy while a large majority of people were still captive of the traditional economic system. Thus, a large majority of the population in the developing world, were betrayed by the engine of modernization and they had no alternative but to retrench themselves into their traditional cultural groups since they found themselves incompatible with the onslaughts of the high technology and the market economic forces.

The market economic forces were so strong that even they did not spare the socialist countries where the State autonomous machinery developed cracks and soon started crumbling under their heavyweight. This gave a blow to the dependency theorists propagating development through people's revolution and state intervention in these nations. Even, people were disenchanted with the political-economy model of development. Further, enamelled by the consumerism of the market economy, orchestrarized by the information revolution and communication networks, they found these changes not in consistency with their values. Consequently, they reorganized themselves around their cultural identities since they considered these as more secure for them than the formal settings.

In the above backdrop, market economy is emerging as a strong accelerating force for globalization. However, increasing political conflicts, inadequate institutional apparatuses, non-prioritization of issues and purposes, local and regional contexts and interests and non-cooperation among nations, appear to be some of the stumbling blocks in its realization. Thus the cultural groupings in the developed and in the developing world are getting accentuated as a reaction to the fractured globalization process.

Another redeeming feature in the resurgence of ethnic identities at the global level is the strong cultural sensitivity to which all groups are subjected. Culture is encompassing and in a sense is a reflection of nature. Contact of technology created by Man with Nature creates culture and groups emerge to regulate their behaviour patterns through the establishment of certain norms and values. Any perceptive understanding of culture, will demand examining "culture for the people" as well as "culture by the people". In the former sense, culture plays a deterministic role in establishing behaviour patterns of people through the indoctrination of norms and values while in the latter sense, Men are seen as rational human beings creating meaningful responses out of the available alternative stimuli and generating behaviour patterns conducive to emerging settings, situations and contexts. In the globalization process, "culture by the people" was limited to a small segment of the population and because of its weak instrumentalities and expressiveness, it could not strike roots with a large majority of the people. On the other hand, "culture for the people" accommodated and comforted all those who got marginalized, alienated, pauperized, disprivileged and discriminated by the market economic forces, triggered by the processes of globalization. As a reaction to this, many of them in response to cultural sensitivity found human symbols and codes created by them for their social existence and survival as more security prone. As such, ethnic identities based on cultural groupings, and primordial ties such as territory, language, kinship, religion, etc., became more pronounced in the post modern era.

In the wake of above emerging situations, perhaps ethno development perspective based on grassroot socio-political movements and popular culture through the involvement of the invisible world of NGOs, may appear to be a suitable strategy for national and global development. However, there is a need to ensure that these ethnic groups are not exploited by the political parties as vote banks for their elections. But before political liberties are ensured, these groups need economic liberties.

Global Solidarity: One World or Several

Solidarity in sociological parlance would represent a system of structures in which the institutionalized ends and values become common and ultimate. This is represented in the societal system by certain kinds of bonds, linkages, networks based on consensus for the accomplishment of desired goals or ends through institutionalized means. For global solidarity, there ought to be sharing of certain bonds and values for achieving the desired goals of peace, progress and prosperity of mankind on this planet. These are lofty goals and require concerned efforts of the nation-States governing this planet. In this direction, the role of United Nations, as an international organization for the promotion of peace, and development is significant. Of about 204 countries on this planet, as many as 180 are members of the UN till February 1993 while nine countries are still non-members but are hoping to be members soon. (The Statemen's Year-Book, 1993). However according to Guiness Book of Records (1993) there are 188 sovereign nations while 61 are non-sovereign nations, that is dependencies of sovereign States, territories claimed in Antarctica and disputed territories as in May 1992. So in all, there are 249 countries.

But after the fall of the USSR, a superpower and that of socialist Second World of Eastern Europe, the UN as an international organ is becoming less effective in bringing peace and development at the global level. Even the fall of the Second World and disintegration of the same into separate nations called into question the rationale behind the term "Third World" as many of the former socialist States of Central and Eastern Europe have now started sharing many common social and economic features with the nations of the Third World. It is observed that the manner in which the people of the former Soviet bloc embraced market forces, is demonstrative of the superiority of the Western capitalism and liberal democracy (Williams, 1993). Further, the Third World nations which had followed a mixed economic path, a part of socialism and a part of capitalism, got the worst of both the worlds and are also now opening themselves more vigorously than before towards the market forces.

Notwithstanding these changes at the global level, the World has been fractured into more parts than it was before due to ethnic resurgences, strifes and conflicts leading to disturbance of peace and escalation of fights, battles and wars on the streets of these fragmented nations. The peace dividends, which have come as a bonus to humanity after the end of forty years of cold war between two super blocs, (cold war had raised the arms expenditure during this period to the tune of $1000 billion annually and of which the Third World share was also 160 billion annually) have not been diverted to improve the lot of the needy, the poor, the malnourished, the disprivileged and the discriminated mass of humanity. It is estimated that of about six billion people on this planet, nearly one billion of them are living in absolute poverty and it is necessary to protect and develop them to tackle the problems of global economic and environmental sustainability.

Changes at the global level seem to have been more dramatic during the last five years than they have been since the post war period. On one side, there has been a return to ethnic identities like tribalism in erstwhile USSR, communalism in India, ethnicism in Sri Lanka and other forms of ethnic coalitions in most parts of the world, especially among the Croats, Serbs and Bosnians and Yugoslaves. However, on the other hand, we have witnessed political as well as economic coalitions of the American and Western European nations against some countries (especially Iraq) for the Gulf War as well as for the unification of European Common Market currency for trade and commerce. Apart from the U.S.A., Germany despite its unification problems with its Eastern part, is emerging as a leader of the European Economic Market. Japan in Asia is another industrial giant and is competing with the USA on the economic front. China in its southern part has also opened up to the market forces while India has also gone in for the liberalized economic reforms to step up her growth potentials. So instead of a unipolar economic power structure of the U.S.A., there is also the emergence of other centres of capitalist growth. In the wake of Western Capitalism and liberal democracy supremacy over socialism at the global level, the main question is whether they shall help the developing world to tackle their problems of poverty, population and environmental sustainability and establish bonds and values for a negotiated understanding and integration or not, in order to establish the global solidarity.

In view of increasing global interdependency and expansion of market forces, there is a feeling of the subordination of the world's diversity to the rationality of market. This premise may lead to the disintegration of the world system and to the renewal of bi-polarization as the market by itself will only reproduce and deepen the contrasts. This fact is being ignored by the ideological legitimization of neo-liberalism. As such, instead of pentapolar political system replacing military bi-polarity reduced to the five "Giants" (the USA, Europe, USSR, China and Japan), Amin opts for polycentrism, allowing for the development of regions and countries of the Third World. To him, a new critical thought should reject dogmatism and propose polycentrism as the only realistic principle to take into account the diversity of conditions and problems of different nations (economically, socially and culturally) for a united world through respect of all people's values (Amin, 1991). This ideal may be difficult to achieve in reality but a beginning can be marked in this direction.

Issues of Global Development

Issues of development have to be contextualized in the world scenario as they are acquiring new meanings and call for joint efforts to meet these challenges. In the North, or in the developed world, there is a challenge of governability because of the problem of certain special interest groups while in the South or in the developing world, there is more of tribal or ethnic problem. Another major challenge faced by both set of countries is the spread of an ideology of liberal democracy in a world fraught with economic inequalities. Further, environmental sustainability is necessary so that all human groups on the planet may enjoy the standards of living equal to that of the industrialized countries. However, due to scarcity and depletion of resources of this planet, competition is deepening and promoting political, economic and cultural conflicts (Arzipe, 1991).

Further, it is observed that sovereignty and non-interference in the internal affairs of the States are the main challenges to be tackled by the international community. Besides, mounting internal conflicts and consequent claim for self-determination by the people to organize themselves into various republics, and collective security for peace making and peace keeping are some of the other challenges to be faced by the people of the world (Otunnu, 1992). Three main crisis, namely, continuing existence of poverty on a large scale, a threat to the natural environment and the resource base, and continuing rapid population growth interacting both with poverty and the environmental damage, affect not only the developing countries but also the chances of survival of human beings on this planet in the next century (Sadik, 1991).

There are certain issues of global development which cannot be tackled within national boundaries and only intervention of international community can provide solution. For example, issues of environment, issues of health epidemics (such as AIDS), terrorism, drug pedalling, may fall into this category. The second set of issues, through not objective, may be considered at the normative level. These pertain to the question of humanitarianism and human rights, equity, justice, democratic standards having universal values, etc. Besides, the issue of solidarity in the world through international cooperation and inclusion of the developing nations into the mainstream capitalism and liberalism, as the International Economic Darwinism fostering competition may scare the weak States and lead to their exclusion, needs to be practiced rather than preached (Otunnu, 1992). Even at the national level, the uneven inclusion of certain ethnic groups into the core society has been observed and this weakens the solidarity dimension of a civil society (Mehta, 1989).

Browsing through the above issues, one can discern clearly the overriding importance of issues related to environmental sustainability, economic and political liberation while certain socio-cultural issues are also emerging. These need to be integrated with the other issues for a global development strategy. An attempt is made in the next section to view global development in the context of cultural values.

Global Development and Culture: A Value Perspective

According to Childe, progress is real if discontinuous (Childe, 1957). Globe has also witnessed numerous changes representing ups and downs while passing through various vicissitudes of its existence. The term global has to be conceived more in terms of having common human goals and to direct changes towards some negotiated understandings providing a bridge between us and a sustainable future, than being viewed as a mask to cover the gaps of "Several Worlds" especially that between the North and the South. On this planet, human systems are characterized by differential levels of economic development and in many cultures, natural world is viewed as opposed to social world. It is in this context that at present, global change is analysed more so in natural than social world through categories of "geosphere" and "biosphere". The third term of "hoo sphere" has been lost sight of in the rationalistic science since this represents the mental or spiritual reality (These terms are given by Russian author Vernadsky). Although "sociosphere" as opposed to "geosphere" and "biosphere" is invisible but as conscious social actors responsible for inventing our history, we have to show our ability to use the finite resources of the planet in a rational sustainable way. This calls for a balancing between "geosphere", "biosphere" and "sociosphere" in order to do an analysis of the global change (Arizpe, 1991).

Martin Price advocates rightly so a need to include a socio-centric perspective along with the other two (geocentric and biocentric) to focus on a new kind of phenomenon such on global economy and a new perspective on world reality that is, to think "globally" or to a new "stage" in world civilization or to a new kind of knowledge, that is, a new global science (Price, 1991). This would necessitate tackling problems such as poverty, population growth and sustainable environment at the global level within a socio-cultural perspective, more close to the world social reality by "Putting People First" in the analysis on global development and through wider sharing of values across nations.

A World of Difference Report of the Netherlands Government, has highlighted that to end poverty (one billion people in absolute poverty), industrial production must increase five to ten fold in the next fifty years, and to make it sustainable, the technologies employed must be five to ten times more efficient than today and a limit shall have to be placed both on population growth and on the scale of production to ensure a sustainable environment. For, effective global change, there is a need to rethink about the concept of national sovereignity, nature of governance, military intervention and expenditure, international trade regulations, debt concessions or waiving, environmental demands of the industrialized nations, the role of the government and the ways and means of mobilizing the human resources and about relating development to one's own institutions and values (Sadik, 1991).

Further, it has been argued that in the years to come, solidarity is a basic necessity and is foundational for building international cooperation through arriving at consensus on what needs to be done. This international cooperation cannot be achieved without building up new institutions and strengthening the existing ones to serve new purposes and urgency of the situations. In fact, we need to have determination to see that these institutions work. A change in economic theory from growth centred paradigm to distribution model is what is desirable in securing greater rationality and equity in establishing relationships between nations and between groups within nations (Claus, 1991).

It is observed that no society can remain isolated in the present world. The new global awareness is establishing a new kind of accountability which will help us establish clear consensual goals and hence new values. The new value system may not lead to the formation of global culture but may set a task for the community of thinkers, decision-makers and organizers for global development. There is a need to create overarching values that may respect local cultures but may provide common goals for all human beings. Besides local economic, social and demographic demands should also be compatible with global imperatives and there is a need to work through conflicts towards concerted actions, better governance, equity and emergence of new cultures in the future (Arizpe, 1992).

While discussing the cultural dimension of sustainability in agricultural development and development in general, the role of values, norms and the relationship between organization and norm enforcement, has been highlighted by Cernea. These regulate the productive activities of people differently across cultures as people in subsistence economies will perceive differently what is advantageous or detrimental to them than those in market economies. This will set limits for laying priorities of needs, goals and values for people in different economic settings. There is a need to work for the cultivation of rationally economic behaviours in consistent with such norms and values for the development purposes (Cernea, 1993).

Notwithstanding the above observations on global development, the role of United Nations and other Third World coalitions like non-aligned movement, Group of 77 and SAARC etc. cannot be ruled out in this direction. For sustainable development of the globe, the suggested essentials are: (a) civil stability, a benign external environment, democratic government and minimal arms expenditure, (b) adequate infrastructure and social services, (c) appropriate population policy, (d) food production, storage and ability to purchase food, (e) forest, water and soil conservation; renewable energy resources and spatially planned development and (f) a stable and equitable external trading and financial environment to foster and sustain all of the above (Childers and Urquhart, 1991). The thrust in the above approach appears to be on technological, institutional, infra-structural, participative and social service oriented changes (Mehta, 1984).

In short, one may say that for the development of the present world without affecting the future, apart from taking into account the "geosphere", "biosphere" technological innovations and infrastructural aspects, a value perspective on global development should focus on creating values pertaining to solidarity through consensus building mechanism, cooperation, institution building, freedom of expression, distributive justice, humanitarianism and human right, liberty in participation, equity and gender equality, etc. A step towards this kind of social and cultural development, thus may become conducive to economic development so necessary for human survival and well-being. Media of communication in this respect can play a significant role in globalizing the minds and in creating cultural idioms, images, themes and symbols that bring progress, happiness and harmony among people and reduce tensions, conflicts, discrimination, deprivation and alienation among the majority on this planet (Mehta, 1992).

We have knowledge affluence in the developed world but information poverty in the developing world. This process has to be reversed through cultural development. Global development shall remain incomplete without the creation of new values. This message should be clearly understood and perceived by the community of international leaders and organizations otherwise the drift between the developed and the developing worlds will increase. We shall then have a fractured and a fragmented world and this will make the living of our future generations difficult. The only alternative shall be to have people's agenda and people's action through negotiated understanding as guiding principles in the value perspective on sustainable global development.

References

Amin, Samir, (1991), "In Favour of Polycentric World", *Development*, Rome Journal of the Society for International Development, 1, pp. 83-85.

Arizpe, Lourdes, (1991), *A Global Perspective to Build a Sustainable Future, Development*, Rome Journal of the Society for International Development, 3/4, pp. 7-9.

Arizpe, Lourdes, (1992), *Ethnicity, Nations and Culture, Development, Rome Journal of the Society for International Development*, 4, pp. 6-8.

Cernea, Michael, M., (1993), *Culture and Organization : The Social Sustainability of Induced Development, Sustainable Development*, Vol. 1, No. 2, pp. 18-29.

Childe, Gordon, (1957), *What-Happened in History,* Harmondsnorth, Middlesex, U.S.A. Penguin Books Ltd., (Reprinted) p. 282.

Childers Erskine, Urquhart, Brian, (1991), *Towards a More Effective United Nations, Development Dialogue,* Sweden Dag Hammarskjold Foundation, 1-2, p. 55.

Claus, Prince H.R.H., (1991), *One World or Many, Development,* Rome Journal of the Society for International Development, 2, pp. 7-11.

Guiness Book of Records, (1993) (edition), Guiness Publishing, U.K., p. 372.

Hamelink, Cees, (1990), "Global Communications: A Plea For Civil Action", 'FENIX', Amesterdam, Friends of Ideas and Action Foundation No. 00.

Mehta, S.R., (1984), *Rural Development Policies and Programmes: A Sociological Perspective,* New Delhi Sage Publications Pvt. Ltd.

Mehta, S.R., (1989), "The Uneven Inclusion of Indian Immigrants in Mauritius", *Sociological Bulletin,* 38(1), March.

Mehta, S.R., (1992), *Communication in Social Development: Issues and Perspectives in Communication and Development* edited by Mehta, S. R., Jaipur Rawat Publications, pp. 1-34.

Otunnu, Olara, (1992), *Emerging Trends in the New World Situations, The Round Table,* The Commonwealth Journal of International Affairs, Issue 324, (October) pp. 401-10.

Price, M., (1991), *Global Change Committee,* Social Science Council, UNU and UNESCO as quoted by Arizpe, Lourdes in "A Global Perspective to Build a Sustainable Future", *Op. cit.,* pp. 7-9.

Sadik, Nafis, (1991), The Barbara Ward Lecture, "Rethinking Modernism: Towards Human Centred Development", *Development,* Rome, Journal of the Society for International Development, 2, pp. 15-20.

Servaes, Jan, (1986), *Communication and Development Paradigms:* An Overview, *Media Asia,* Vol. 13, No. 3.

StatesMan's Year Book, (1993-94), (1993). 130th edition, London MacMillan Press, pp. 7-8.

Williams Marc, (1993), *Re-artifulating the Third World Coalition. The Role of the Environmental Agenda, Third World Quarterly,* Journal of the Emerging Areas, Vol. 14, No. 1.

World of Difference Report, (1991), *Netherlands Government as quoted in Sadik Nafis,* "Rethinking Modernism: Towards Human Centred Development", *Ibid.*

8

Communication and Development

At the present juncture, communication processes and strategies of development of developing nations are encountering many odds. Communication is indispensable to development. But we do not have adequate knowledge in regard to how development plans of these nations should recognize and utilize this indispensable element in changing minds and developing appropriate attitudes and thought patterns of their people for making or triggering off the phenomenon of development.

Communication is an essential process of social life which is both interactive and purposeful. Throughout the history, it has facilitated in binding people and bringing them together to make it possible to have a social life through increasing their susceptibility to suggestions and initiations and by guiding them to take appropriate actions. However, it is also observed that communication concepts and methods cannot be meaningfully considered without taking into account the developmental perspectives and ideologies in which these operate.

Development is a dynamic concept of a stable society while growth and structural changes are its implicit or explicit goals (Mehta, 1984). It is suggested that no action is possible without ideological underpinning and one cannot adequately choose between alternative actions without an understanding of the nature of beliefs that make them. (Bailey, 1975). Ideology ascribes motives to particular people and groups of people which do not stem from a desire for some independent cognitive truth but derive mainly from interest which is reflected in seeing the world to conform to a pre-existing idea held about it, an idea of which one has become convinced independently of the evidence (Merton, 1972). Thus development takes the form or follows the path that ideology of a particular society provides to it. Consequently, the communication strategies will be designed to fit well into the development perspectives or approaches that a nation may opt for.

Though it may be desirable to examine the historical processes of a society which resulted in the development of communication system and networks within it, yet in the contemporary context, it may be more apt to look into the role that communication can play in accelerating the development initiatives of a developing nation. Further, one may like to analyse the communication concepts and methods in the context of both evolutionary and revolutionary perspectives of development, though in the Indian setting evolutionary framework may be more appropriate than the latter. Before analysing these, it may be desirable to discuss briefly the phenomenon of communication and highlight the various perspectives of human communication along with those of development.

Communication Phenomenon and Perspectives

Communication is often considered as a means for breaking down the barriers to human interaction and for achieving mutual understanding between persons. Communication as a phenomenon is ubiquitous and equivocal. It remains constant, though our understanding of it changes. It is observed that communication as a process is variable only as a function of one's theoretical or conceptual perspective, otherwise it remains same, no matter at what sociological level or setting it occurs—interpersonal or societal. In other words, communication—the phenomenon, itself is not problematic, only human understanding of it is problematic (Fischer, 1978).

A brief account of four major perspectives of human communication is presented here for adequate understanding of the phenomenon of communication. The mechanistic perspective emphasizes on the transmission process of information or message through socially organized channels and on the mechanistic interpretation of such a message. The psychological perspective, on the other hand, lays stress on reception as well as production of stimuli in the informational environment where each communicator is psychologically oriented to one another.

Besides, the communicative situation is characterized by a structural stimulus field and a certain degree of purposes on the part of the communicator; the stimulus field having been structured after taking into account the response structure.

The interactional perspective of human communication is 'dialogical' in nature and is based on symbolic interactionism of human beings. The emphasis is on action and symbolic action in a processual development of human communication, allowing role-taking to the development of joint action or linking of individual action with the actions of other individuals to form a collectivity. The last perspective, the pragmatics, based on tenets of system theory, focus on symbols to people relationship that is, symbol to user relationship. This perspective emphasizes on the behaviour of the communicator, which may virtually be synonymous with communication itself. The processing of information is central to this model. It is observed that it is information that energizes the social system and allows the system to survive. When communication occurs in a social system, the individuals are engaged in the processing of information after comprehending it and utilizing it for the stability and persistence of that system, the communicative act being based on the process of choosing out of available alternative types of information within the social system (Fischer, 1978).

While discerning these perspectives on communication, one has to keep in view that these are not mutually exclusive and may be used in combination for developing communication systems in the developing or in the developed world.

Development Perspectives

Development initiatives have assumed greater complexities over the years but broadly we can classify these efforts within the evolutionary, that is, structural functional or revolutionary, that is, conflict or dialectical concepts and methods. It is observed that nations which followed evolutionary approaches to development are showing symptoms of frustration with them and are inclined to adopt revolutionary methods while nations which went in for revolutionary methods are finding them less rewarding and are keen to follow the evolutionary methods of development. This has made development a more difficult and challenging task. The evolutionary perspective on development emphasizes on movement from a less to more differentiated social form through processes of ever more complex specialization and functional interdependence. As societal development proceeds, certain 'adaptive features' are incorporated which increase the capacity of the system to adapt to its environment. Thus integration and adaptation become the two important dimensions of the developmental system. Such a view of development found evidence in the themes on modernization. According to these themes, the concept of development lies in changing the character of individuals, that is, changing the attitudes and values of men to enable them to adapt and promote a modern society (Maclelland, 1967; Hagen, 1962; Lerner, 1965; Alex Inkeles, 1966).

In short, in this perspective on development, enactment of values and the spirit of modernity is regarded both as a pre-consideration for societal modernization and as a major consequence of it (Portes, 1976). Further, it is observed that the ideal of this perspective on development requires the transformation of the nature of Man—a transformation that is a means to the end of yet a greater growth and at the same time one of the great ends itself of the development process (Inkeles, 1966).

Thus, the development of traditional societies into modern ones was a contemporary intellectual extension of social Darwinian evolution (Rogers, 1976). However, this evolutionary perspective on development fell into disrepute as it failed to tackle the problems of development in the developing nations of Asia, Africa and Latin America. Instead the Chinese experience and to a lesser extent that of Cuba, Tanzania and Chile, made the rest of the world to learn details of new pathways to development. This prompted a search for new or alternative pathways to development.

The conflict perspective or dialectical framework of development derives its conceptualization from the Marxist stream of thought. According to this perspective, the basic cause of development is the internal contradictions within a society, that is between forces of production and relations of production resulting in contradictions between classes and between the old and the new structures. It is the development of these contradictions that pushes forward the society and provides impetus for the replacement of the old by the new social order. Thus, in this view of development, external causes are the conditions of change and the internal causes (contradictions) are the bases of change (Marx, 1974).

Following Marx, a number of radical scholars agree that as capitalism advances, the competitive relations of production transform into monopoly relations and the monopolists appropriate most of the means of production in their country and then seize more or less completely the industry of other weaker nations. It is, further, observed that there is a dialectical relationship between development and underdevelopment. The underdevelopment of the developing nations is not because they lack resources, technical knowhow, modern institutions or cultural traits conducive to development but because they are being exploited by the worldwide capitalist system. There is a dependency of periphery on the core countries. These through the intervention of multinationals are trying to eliminate the native industries and destroy the internal creativity inherent in national traditions of periphery nations. According to this perspective, development is possible only if an exploited nation can free itself both externally and internally from its dependency of the capitalist system.

In short, according to this perspective, development should proceed through a revolutionary process, overthrowing capitalism by socialism, the revolution being stimulated by the contradictions inherent in the capitalist system. However, Andre Gunder Frank, in one of his recent articles advocates a world economic order which he hopes to be uneven and pins faith on revolution as a condition of change of dependency of periphery from core countries but expresses with despair that even the socialist countries which should have moved from socialism to the next stage of communism are getting back to capitalism because of the strong hold of the international capitalist economic system (Frank, 1983).

Both these perspectives of development have been criticized as much for their logical imperfections as for their empirical distortions, apart from their ideological predilections. However, development by both is treated as a normative concept, as almost a synonym for improvement towards a better society (Seers, 1970). The development strategies in both cases aim to achieve economic growth and social, cultural and political transformations of their respective societies by maintaining their positions either as ruling elites or as dictators of the socialist parties, each professing to bring in development by eliminating the discontents prevailing in the other ideological framework. Notwithstanding the merits or demerits of each of these perspectives of development, in the context of developing nations, it is the aspirations and preparation of people which should be the main cause and consequence of economic and social development.

Communication and Development

It is suggested that the structure of social communication reflects the structure and development of a society. The size of the communication activity, the development of mass media and their audiences, the transfer of the individual communication roles of the traditional society to organizations, the stretching out and multiplying of communication channels reflect the economic development of the society. The ownership of communication facilities, the purposeful use of communication, the controls on communication reflect the political development and the philosophy of a given society. Further, the contents of communication reflect the value patterns of the society and the pattern of communication flows and who shares it with whom, reflect the homogeneity of culture within a society. As such, communication is a reflection of the larger patterns of society. (Schramm, 1963). In the light of the above, communication stimulates development in the economic, social, cultural and political spheres.

A brief account of the communication strategies as advocated by the two perspectives of development will provide an insight in to the processes involved in communication and development.

Lerner (1958), basing his premise that modernity is an interactive behavioural system, shows how and why mass media functions in modern and rapidly modernising societies. Mass media like films and radio act as 'mobility multipliers', leading people to an imaginary universe and preparing them psycho-socially for a change while disciplining them in empathic skills by bringing in new aspirations. In the event, that societal institutions outrun the aspirations, mass media work to bring dissatisfaction conceived as frustration, leading either to aggression or regression among people.

In order to avoid regression, Lerner suggests a new conception of public communication combining mass media with school and community leaders, to induce a new process of socialization among the rising generation, especially new participants into the development process. Lerner seems to be overemphasizing the role of mass media in creating new values. This seems to be not substantiated adequately by the studies done by Columbian School (Lazarsfeld, Berelson; Katz, etc.). These studies have emphasized on the two step flow of information from mass media to influentials and from influentials to individuals who do not have access to mass media. In fact, there is enough evidence now available which indicates that interpersonal communication operates as an important mediating factor between stimulus and response in the mass communication process. "Mass communications operating by themselves can be effective in directly making an impact on attention, information, tastes and images but do not, however decisively influence the development of skills, actions and attitudes, unless they are reinforced by other personal agencies" (Pool, 1963). Wilbur Schramm (1964) has been another scholar who advocated that communication bears a peculiarly organic relation to society. According to him, communication system makes industrial development easier and industrial development makes communication development easier. The typical history of communication development shows that it has advanced most in these countries where education, industry, urbanization, national income, political participation and the mass media have all gone forward together stimulating each other, the lagging of one behind the other often resulting in the failure of the societal system. Schramm argues that if 'need achievement' values were developed once in the advanced industrial societies of the West, these can be developed by the mass media in the developing countries as well. He suggests special relationship between schools and mass media in the context of developing nations as each of them has a broad educational task to perform and acts as 'teacher multiplier'. These need to be utilized to evolve strategies of national development without creating excessive needs and frustration. However, this repeats the curious assumption that the western industrial experience is bound to be repeated elsewhere in totally different circumstances; that if something happens once in history, it must necessarily reoccur (Benge, 1972).

Another scholar who stresses the primacy of achievement values for development is McClelland (1961). On the basis of analysing the media content of organized verbal or symbol systems—for example, folk tales or pottery designs, he has deduced national values. The frequency with which certain types of symbolic forms appear in various cultures may be indicative of predicting other cultural phenomena such as forms of religious organization, types of games people play and the rate of economic development. He suggests that where symbols indicate a high concern for achievement in a nation, more rapid economic growth is likely to take place there. Like Lerner, he is advocating new norms for a modern society by replacing the traditional attitudes but his basic assumption that media can create new attitudes or change attitudes as a prerequisite before any other social development, may not be valid in all situations. Moreover, he, like Lerner, has underestimated the role of mediating factor such as interpersonal communication in the effect of mass media.

Marshall McLuhan (1964) postulated another perspective maintaining that a major shift in predominant existing technology of communication is responsible for initiating changes in a society; not only in social organization but in human sensibilities as well. For example, the invention and mass production of printed materials encouraged nationalism by allowing more rapid and wider spread of information than was permitted by hand written messages. Similarly, electric modes of communication—telegraph, radio, television, movies, telephones, computers—are reshaping the civilization in the twentieth century by initiating changes in the direction of sensory awareness of what McLuhan calls 'sensory ratios'.

According to him, 'Societies have been shaped more by the nature of the media by which men communicate than by the 'content of communication' and for him, 'medium is the message' and it is technology of communication that shapes every important aspect of society's life.

The above proposition may be hard to digest as it does not fit into the conventional wisdom. However, McLuhan has expressed that a medium like television demands a 'creative participant response'. But this response must be to the medium itself and not to what is conveyed for, seemingly man need no longer concern for himself with the creative or moral implications of mass media or with value judgements about them. This separation of form from content seems artificial as in communication, they are inseparable. Further the basic assumption which resigns man to become a 'servo-mechano' of electronic technology, is spurious and self-defeating, for it ignores the social implications of mass communication. The effect of mass media become irrelevant if the medium rather than communication content is the message as it is not only the media which have revolutionized but the way in which these have been used. Who says what to whom under what circumstances and with what effect cannot be delegated to the computer alone to determine. The ethical alternatives and the value judgements are inherent in man (Benge, 1972).

An Indian scholar, Kuppuswamy, considers child rearing, education and mass media as three avenues to bring about a reorientation in an individual with a view to developing new outlook and behaviour as a citizen so that social, economic and the political structures of the society are transformed. According to him, the processes of family socialization and education are complementary in development but the Indian youth is in a predicament because of the conflict of the traditional values of the family socialization and the achievement values fostered by education. There is a need to change the primary process of family socialization so as to inculcate the dominant values of the changing society among the children. The gap between the family socialization process of the child and values fostered by education can be bridged by mass media exposure to develop appropriate attitudes among children and youth for development (Kuppuswamy, 1976).

On the other hand, the alternative strategy of communication in development has been vividly presented by Chinese experience. According to this strategy 'There is not a theory of state and theory of communication, but there is only one theory' (Frederick, 1963). In fact, theory and practice of communication in a communist society is the ideology itself. It is observed that solidarity and achievement depend upon ideological unanimity and communications provide the model with which to conform. Therefore, communication becomes as indispensable tool of development in such societies. The entire process of mass persuasion is through people's participation in development programmes and is generally built around a control task of one kind or another. In other words, the policy of communication is synchronized with every task of the party and it is through these tasks that the major objectives of propaganda and mass campaigns are achieved. Although, methods used may vary, yet there are four major stages of intensive type followed in mass campaigns. These are (1) Attention attraction, (2) Ideological preparation, (3) The taking of action and (4) Review of the struggle (Frederick, 1967).

In addition to mass media like films and radio and personal agitation, they also use traditional forms of media such as blackboard, newspapers, posters, street corner plays, folk dances, songs, poetry, operas and mass contributions of every kind. In fact, it is the political policy that makes communication a powerful instrument of change and this makes informal face-to-face communication, the characteristics of mass media system.

There is criticism levelled against both the types of perspectives on communication and development outlined above. Research in many Third World countries, has shown that the communication models or paradigms applied for bringing about social changes have often proved ineffective because of cultural, social, economic and political characteristics prevailing in these nations. It is in fact, westernized elite oriented view of communication unlinked to the word of mouth communication that makes communication ineffective in generating action for development in the Third World countries. It is argued that without an effective political organization at the grass roots levels to provide word of mouth support for the messages in the mass media, the latter do not produce desired action results (Pool, 1963).

Two-step communication involving the interpersonal communication, as a part of mass communication has now been widely accepted by communication experts who seek to make their communication strategies action oriented. Another problem has been that most of the people in these countries despite exodus from the villages, still live in the rural areas. So they are not accessible to the Communication. It is observed that there are two communication systems in developing countries and the ideas and themes dominant in urban or central system are not reflected in the rural areas. In the latter system, important news may travel quickly but interpretation and context do not; nor are the contents of radio and newspapers designed for the villagers and there is no local media (Pye, 1963).

In regard to alternative approach of communication and development, we have evidences to show that Chinese have made most effective use of all communication channels but liberal communication experts think that the cost in human terms was great in transforming the Chinese society. Further they argue that this approach creates a new gap between the manifest level of social communications and people's private and intensely subjective reactions; giving way to a sense of isolation and powerlessness among individuals. The total propaganda in that sense may become counterproductive (Pye, 1963). Another, criticism against this strategy of communication is that it is based on the element of coercion and regimentation. But it is argued that thought control operates all over the underdeveloped world in varying degrees, and nowhere we do find press or radio free of government. (Benge, 1972). However, recent reports on China indicate efforts of the State to set up a television based distant education university and extensive use of mass media for adult education purposes.

Communication Methods and Strategies in India's Development

A country like India with inadequate financial resources, technology and large population size, has no choice but to emphasize an information based human development strategy, if she wishes to develop at a faster pace. Social development becomes possible when people have a wider vision of the society in which they live and of their role in it. This would necessitate a national communication system for understanding the need of the people and for evolving and sharing a consensus on national plans. The efforts in this information intensive human development strategy will have to be, to discover and implement procedures that may effectively train and mobilize the human resources. Development of a communication infrastructure permitting the flow of information throughout a country in that sense is an important prerequisite of development.

In the above backdrop, it may appear imperative to examine communication and development in the Indian context. India is a continental size country with a population of nearly one billion people. Nearly 75 per cent of its population lives in the rural areas and is represented by diverse ethnic, linguistic, religious and socio-cultural groups. Politically she has been directed so far by the democratic forces and economically, her main problems have been poverty, inequality and ignorance or lack of education. The urban metropolitan centres are islands of wealth, richness and extravagance with some pockets of shanty dwellings, insanitary living conditions, poverty and squalor represented by the slum dwellers.

Despite only 25 per cent of the population residing in metropolitan cities and other urban centres, they tend to be the maximum users of communication system as they have the majority of the literate group (nearly 50 per cent of the population of the country is literate) inhabiting these places. Obviously then, the production, distribution and consumption of communication networks, may it be television, radio, newspapers, cinema, etc. are shared most directly or indirectly by the urban dwellers. Consequently, the planning of the communication contents, remains centralized as a byproduct of mainly the urban elite culture.

As a consequence of the above, communications have touched the rural areas in a peripheral manner and have mainly concentrated on informing people within the reach of the media employed to support some urgent national tasks for development. As such, we find that the information flow is weak where it is needed and wherever a distant channel is employed, the original information tends to become distorted. This necessitates supporting mass media approach with media such as posters, leaflets or specific rural radio or T.V. programmes, regional language newspapers or interpersonal communication through change agents in different development initiatives for diffusion and adoption of innovations. This would require efforts and amount of resources that a country like ours would have to generate or look forward to.

Another problem often posed is that communication system in the developing nations should be value relevant whereas programme planners of media in a multi ethnic, linguistic and religious country like ours may find it difficult to match the communication contents and messages through various media to the value framework of diverse people. Conforming to traditions, value orientations and social structural dimensions of people may be desirable element of the communication network but a communication system designed for developmental purposes should also function to affect the attitudes and values of people for a new social order. We have only to be clear about our goals.

In connection with above, the communication system can become more effective, if it could be decentralized with appropriate institution building at local, district, state and regional levels, with a view to have feedback and feedforward mechanisms built into development support communication systems attached to various organizations responsible for developmental work, such as agriculture, health, population, education, youth and women welfare or industry, etc. Decentralization would also envisage strengthening or streamlining the grass root level organizations such as the panchayats, the schools and the cooperatives and revitalizing the village level functionaries as change agents in the field of agriculture, health, family planning and education, to make word to mouth or interpersonal communication as a part of the mass communication system.

These efforts will also help in building a communication system relevant to value patterns of people in different regions and at the same time, bringing forth the national development tasks before them for integration and cohesion. Such an information system will also be built up from bottom upwards for a more realistic planning based on audience response. However, such a decentralized approach in the communication system would expect better commitment of community leadership to mediate the interpersonal communication in the mass media strategy. Necessary infrastructure and hardware communication technologies appropriate to the regional development of various states will have to be well thought of in the communication system. However, from the sociological point of view, what is important is the software in the communication network, that is, audience response and evaluation. Instead of making communication messages more mechanistic and deterministic, the focus shall have to be shifted from the structure of stimulus to response side and treating them more humanistic in nature and form.

Communication as a process should be continuous and aim at raising the hopes, aspirations and tastes of the people so that they would build up behaviours appropriate to development initiatives but communication as a strategy of development should focus, apart from others, on certain target groups such as youth, women and landless especially in the rural areas. The aspirations raised of the people should be fulfilled by providing means to them so that these, if remained unfulfilled may not lead to frustrations resulting either in aggressive or regressive behaviour, counterproductive to the development efforts.

Our communication experts have failed to design strategies which could raise the tastes and aspiration levels of the poor and underprivileged groups such as landless labourers, women and youth in the rural areas. As such, they have developed apathy, indifference, submissiveness and resignation to forces beyond their control and this has perpetuating influence on their 'poverty' and 'community of fate' attitude. This lack of fit of the communication system into the value framework of such people would necessitate shaking them vigorously and helping them to realize and make efforts for bettering their living conditions. The information system must be geared to sensitize such target groups for generating new attitudes and values among them and in removing their fears, doubts and apprehensions regarding developmental issues.

In this above endeavour, apart from communication system,

there is a need to supplement the efforts through educational initiatives of both formal and non-formal type. Formal schooling system needs to be run on making our villagers farm management oriented and for vocationalising them to take up certain self-employment avenues. Education coupled with communication media of different variety may sensitize the poor and underprivileged groups to acquire better tastes for themselves and for their families.

The commercialization of media such as television, radio and newspapers have made people more consumption oriented. Though the efforts may be to boost up the market for the goods produced through the advertising world, yet the revenue earned from these sources, unless invested in productive pursuits or programmes of a developmental nature, may prove counter productive and anti-developmental as these efforts may raise demands rather than satisfy human needs. When demands tend to become the needs of the people, these often result in providing false modernization effects (Mehta, 1981). This may require steps to curb down consumerism and encourage savings among people.

Communication process does not necessarily mean total rejection of traditional and acquiring of modern values but it would have better effects if the traditional values are stated explicitly and assessed or evaluated along with the modern values for modernization and development of people. For development of the people, participatory communication strategy will have to be evolved so that people would go beyond the realm of modernization and energise information to activate themselves in action oriented schemes or project of productive nature. Their commitment to development will be more if they are actively involved in it.

The most difficult and challenging task is to conceive and design the communication contents as even if one assumes that medium is the message, the communication effects are reflected through the media contents which may constitute a judicious mix of entertainment, recreation, local, national and international events, education, health, population, agriculture, industry, youth and women activities or other development initiatives. Thus programme planning behind the scene involves tremendous task and needs to be developed after taking into account the feedback and evaluation of the audience.

Efforts should be to reduce the communication effect gap among persons of different socio-economic groups or by having specialized information for particular groups. Of the important mass media, television and cable network is a costly gadget which people in rural India can hardly afford; radio, especially the transistorized sets have become increasingly accessible to rural people even in areas where there is no electricity but the audience has confined itself mainly to music and entertainment part of it. Newspapers, unless these are developed in regional languages as a part of rural press, have hardly any utility for the villagers. Cinematography which draws a large number of commuters from villages to urban centres need to be installed in the villages by having more of mobile talkies or locating these in places very close to rural areas. The VCR which provides a threat to cinema in the urban centres can be effectively used as a substitute for cinema in the villages. The limited approach of such media in the rural areas need revitalization and utilization of traditional media of communication such as puppetry, folksongs, drama or folk plays, religious songs, etc., in disseminating information to the disadvantaged groups of the society. These can be effectively combined by change agents in their efforts of word to mouth communication strategy.

Thus a communication system in the Indian context will have to be evolved at two levels. First, it will have to consist of highly organized or explicitly structured mass media. Secondly, informal opinion leaders or change agents who communicate on face to face basis, similar to a communication process that existed in the traditional system, will have to be mobilized. In other words, in the context of developing countries such as India, where a vast majority of the population live in villages and are illiterate, communication strategies will have to assume a role of educating the masses through the mediated approach of interpersonal communication by the change agents in different sectors of development. Even the contents of mass media for rural people will have to be evolved independently of their urban counterparts.

Conceptually speaking in our context, it may be worthwhile

to combine the mechanistic model of communication with the interactional perspective emphasing empathy as a link between the individuals or groups with a possibility of instantaneous or immediate feedback. Even in the combining of mechanistic model with the psychological perspective of human communication, one has to discern that while preparing the communication contents, the emphasis has to be on the stimulus side so that the feedback mechanism could become more effective in developing an empathy of communicative relationship among actors. The information thus diffused between actors at different levels of the system may help in energising it for its adequate functioning. The pragmatics or the system perspective of communication becomes more important when information is to be processed as it energizes the system and thereby provides an opportunity for decision making at the national level.

The use of compulsion, force or coercion to influence individuals or groups for decisionmaking, as propogated by communists, is not applicable in our situation. The caste system is peculiar to our country and religious values do not allow suppression. Change associated with education is more self-sustained and we should bring it by informing others and discussing with them so that it is socially acceptable. However, the control of capitalists on communication through mass media should be checked and the nation State should evolve a suitable communication policy and strategy to solve the developmental problems of the rural poor, especially that of landless labourers, youth and women.

References

Bailey, Joe, (1975), *Social Theory for Planning,* London, Routedge and Kegan Paul.

Bange, Ronald C., (1972), *Communication and Identity,* London, Clive Bingley.

Fischer, Aubrey, (1978), *Perspectives on Human Communications,* New York, MacMillan Publishing Co.

Frank, Andre Gunder, (1983), "Crisis and Transformation of Dependency in the World-System", in Ronald H. Chilcote and Dale L. Johnson (eds.), *Theories of Development,* Beverly Hills Sage

Publications.

Frederick, T. C. Yu, (1963), "Communications and Politics in Communist China", in Lucian W. Pye (ed), *Communications and Political Development*, New Jersey, Princeton University Press.

———, (1967) in Lerner and Schramm (ed.), *Communication and Change in Developing Countries*, Honolulu, East-West Centre Press.

Hagen, Everett E., (1962), *On the Theory of Social Change*, Illinois, Homewood, Dorsey.

Inkeles, Alex, (1966), "The Modernization of Man" in Myron Weiner (ed), *Modernization : The Dynamics of Growth*, New York, Barie.

Katz, Elihn, (1957), "The Two Step Flow of Communication", *Public Opinion Quarterly*, 21, No. 1.

Kuppuswamy, B., (1976), *Communication and Social Development in India*, New Delhi, Sterling Publishers.

Larner, Daniel, (1958), *The Passing of Traditional Society, Modernising the Middle East*, New York, Free Press.

Lazarsfeld, P.F. et al, (1944), *The People's Choice*, N.Y., Columbia University Press.

Marx, Karl, (1974), *Capital: A Critique of Political Economy*, Vol. III, (Fifth Impression), Moscow, Progress Publishers.

McClelland, David G., (1967), *The Achieving Society*, N.Y, Free Press.

McLuhan, Marshall H., (1964), *Understanding Media: The Extensions of Man*, N. Y., McGraw Hill Co.

Mehta, S.R., (1981), *Rural Development Programmes and Policies: A Sociological Perspective*, New Delhi, Sage Publications.

———, (1984), *Social Development in Mauritius: A Study on Rural Modernization in an Island Community*, New Delhi, Wiley Eastern Ltd.

Merton, R.K., (1972), "Insiders and Outsiders : A Chapter in the Sociology of Knowledge", *American Journal of Sociology*, 78.

Pool, Ithiel De Sola, (1963), "Mass Media and Politics in Modernization Process" in Lucian W. Pye (ed.) *Communications and Political Development*, New Jersey, Princeton University Press.

Portes, Alejandro, (1976), "On the Sociology of National Development: Theories and Issues", *American Journal of Sociology*, 82.

Pye, Lucian W., (1963), *Communications and Political Development*, New Jersey, Princeton University Press.

Rogers, Everett M. (ed.), (1982), *Communication and Development: Critical Perspectives*, Beverly Hills, London, Sage Publications.

Schramm Wilbur, (1963), *Mass Media and National Development*, Standford, Standford University Press.

———, (1964), "Communication Development and the Development Process" in Lucian W. Pye (ed.), *Communications and Political Development*, *op. cit.*

Seers, Dudley, (1970), "The Meaning of Development", *The Agricultural Development Council Reprint.*

9

Democratization of Communication for Development

India is a democratic country. As a developing country, she has, as yet, to acquire the basic expressions of a democracy. These have been identified as lack of exploitation, equalization, generalized popular participation, the dignity of employment, adequate income, individual and social creativity (Somavia, 1981). However, in its preamble, the Constitution of India has laid down social justice, equality and fraternity as basic goals to be accomplished through democratic means.

All political systems committed to democracy are seeking various combination of political, social, economic and cultural democracy but in reality, they do not have a satisfactory arrangement. There are variations shown within a democratic system which are often related to varying social and political structures. Some democratic systems may consider health and education as functions of income while others may treat them as functions of human rights. Again, for certain social systems, the concentration of wealth in a few hands can coexist with extreme poverty situations without affecting the fabric of democracy while for others, democracy implies elimination of extreme wealth as well as poverty (Somavia, 1981).

The decade of 1990s has ushered in democracy all over the world. Communication and information revolution has resulted in the fall of socialist regimes and even communist nations have opened up to new market economic forces. With the ending of the cold war, the bipolar power structure has given way to a unipolar capitalist power system. However, within the capitalist system, there is emergence of new economic centres such as Japan in Asia, unified Germany in Europe besides USA, and most of all the EEC (European Economic community nowadays known as the European Union). These new realities have promoted transnational economic enterprises which demand international laws related to freedom of economic enterprise, liberty of political representation and ecological and environmental preservation problems.

Market economy may not be a panacea for all developmental problems of the developed and the developing world but it has an overwhelming influence even over the socialist or communist nations. Local or regional socio-cultural, economic and political considerations have to be given serious considerations for development of the developing nations besides free market economic forces.

The fallouts of market economic forces are severe for developing nations. There is cultural mediation of these affluent nations and they tend to dominate not only in economic, military and political but in cultural spheres as well. Cultural conquest rather than cultural cooperation is the order of the day. The question is whether in this background, it is possible for people in the developing nations to get an opportunity to make their own lives and at the same time challenge the confines of the State and economic institutions to find a space for themselves or not. Further, it is to be seen whether it is possible to establish a new information and communication order based on free and direct flow of information, accountability to public, capacity of societies and individuals to control their own destinies, mutual exchange through horizontal interactions and appropriate use of new technologies.

These questions rightly raise the issue posed in one of the seminar papers: What kind of communication for what kind of development? Notwithstanding the constraints of international economic, political and military order, India shall have to evolve a self-regulating system of communication within before she opens up her communication with the South and the North for a world communication order. Cultural diversity in terms of language, dialect, ethnic and caste groups, geographical locations of people and religious beliefs, makes development communication in this country of continental size, a difficult and challenging proposition.

Before we could think of communication strategy for India's development, it may be worthwhile to examine first the development issues that need rapt attention. Poverty, ignorance, unemployment and underemployment, population growth and shelter, are the major problems to be tackled through development initiatives in our country. Development planners followed a mixed economic approach (equal emphasis on private and public sectors) for industrial growth and technological package for increased agricultural production in order to tackle some of the above mentioned problems besides emphasising social services such as education, health, population control, youth and women welfare and housing schemes. The resultant outcome of nearly five decades of development planning is widening gaps in income of people despite increased production, large proportion of people in the poverty group, poor health, malnutrition, and widespread illiteracy.

Market economic forces over the years became dominant and promoted consumerism whereas the objectives related to social responsibility and human rights as provided in the Constitution and as envisioned by our national leadership after independence of the country, were paid lip service. As a consequence, oppression, discrimination and alienation of the weaker sections of the society became the visible features. Social responsibility and human rights became subservient to economic gains and the outcome of this development was corruption, nepotism, red tapeism, crimes of different types, violence, murder, threat to life, and exploitation in its varied forms. The politicians further added fire to the fuel and during the last two years, in their election manifestos, they promoted and projected development issues related to "Mandal", "Masjid', "Ram Janam Bhoomi", "Liberalization", "Privatization", etc., than even a "Garibi Hatao" slogan and created more chaos and confusion for the voters. The minority government at the centre, being non-functional and considering the nature of polity in this country, political instability observed during the last few years may further lead to maldevelopment. The political system apart from being commercialized is becoming communalized and criminalized. Under such circumstances, there is much despair than hope for the development of the country.

In India, we have a two-tier economy, one fast moving fuelled and propelled by high level technological transfer. This has marginalized a majority of our population and forced them to retrench themselves into their traditional way of life. The second is our traditional village economy which is no longer self-contained and is subject to stresses and strains of modern life. The nation-state, at no cost is willing to part with technological advancement as in that case, we will be left behind in the development race because modernization of our infrastructure is necessary for development purposes. This sets limits on them to allocate resources for the upliftment of rural people. Further, our social fabric stands torn and shorn due to the onslaughts of modernizing forces. In fact our values and value orientations have been diffused and shaken to a large extent.

In the above scenario of our country, where our politico-economic and socio-cultural fabrics are cracking down, what could be the strategy of communication for development? If Congress (I) in its election campaign had made Rajiv Gandhi synonymous with development through the slogan *Vikas Ki Aandhi Rajiv Gandhi* one starts wondering, what sort of values our political media is promoting. At the affective level, such a synonymity may have an emotive appeal but at the cognitive level, *aandhi* (dust storm) may convey contradictory signal of 'sweeping people off the development" while at the connotative level, it is probabilistic and does not assure of an affirmative action.

This warrants examining the relevance of media to our cultural idioms, ethos and moorings. Media of communication are productions of our culture and technology. Technology conditions environment and vice versa, the contact between the two leads to the growth of culture. Media, as a part of culture, have to promote through projection, the images of Man's interest, contributive and distributive justice, freedom of expression, liberty in participation and emancipation from obstructionism, superstitions and magico-religious practices. In short, media have to operate within the value framework of a society.

As such, the cultural production factories manufacturing

media through appropriate technologies, must be based on the value system prevalent in our society. If the development needs or goals are to focus on equality, social justice, fraternity among people, then the media projection on "Privatization", "Mandir" and "Masjid" may send contradictory images to the people and the development initiatives to remove or reduce oppression, discrimination and alienation among the weaker sections of the society may boomerang the development efforts. Again, the populist cultural serials televised on television and broadcast through radio, are in no way close to the values upheld in our society or to the values desired in the society for social harmony and integration. Advertisements in heavy dozes have in fact, eroded our cultural ethos and promoted consumerism among the people. Newspapers give precedence to political than development news. Films depict more of fantacies than social problems and are cheap source of entertainment. Commercial art has replaced our traditional art and culture and media or communications have ineffectively touched the problems of poverty, malnutrition, health, population control, unemployment, migration, untouchability, widow remarriage, status of women, eradication of illiteracy, land reforms and reservation policy so crucial for our development.

In development communication, media strategy should be to base the media of communication on the values inherent in our social structure and simultaneously alter the value orientations of our people so as to restructure and change the social system through establishing credible and appropriate interactions with the people.

This raises another question as to who will handle values prevalent in our social system with dynamism and provide policy leads for planning and implementation of development communication strategies? This brings into, the question of "Media organizations" and "Media men". These have to operate within the framework of development planning adopted in our country. If the development goals are to be achieved through the function of "income" and "privatization", then the development objectives of social justice, equality and fraternity shall have to bid good-bye to our constitution, and social responsibility and human rights as function of development shall have to be side-tracked. Our political masters will have to take hard decisions on restructuring and revising our constitution otherwise they will fall into the trap of getting the worst of both the capitalist and the socialist approaches in our development planning. Let us be clear in our vision about the goals of development in our society.

Assuming that our political masters will take more pragmatic than drastic approaches, our media organizations need to be decentralized and taken away from the centres of power. It is only in this way that they can relate media to our value system. By making these values as base, they can stimulate certain values desired in the context of our development goals and create a new social structure for our society. Depending upon the nature and form of media messages, media contents need to be developed in specialized media organizations which should have autonomous structures while having public accountability built into them.

Democratization of media of communication can become effective only if financial autonomy is accorded to media organizations. Public funding rather than that by powerful economic and financial groups can only sustain communication for social development, otherwise it will tend to operate at the industrial level. Advertising by powerful economic groups in an industrialized economy is the major source of revenue for funding the communication organizations.

For democratization of communication, certain limits shall have to be set for the contribution of advertising in the overall funding of media, besides rational distribution of advertising among different media and providing public subsidies in the field of education and health. Public funding, as in Sweden, can go a long way in providing freedom of expression and pluralism in communication structures. Public funding can also be augmented by taxation on advertising outlays or imports of foreign communication materials, provisions in national budgets and support through international sources (Somavia, 1981). Political control and that by bureaucrats should be replaced by a Board of Governors and Directors, which should be accountable to public organizations and forums. Rewards and facilities have to be built into the organizational system so as to provide suitable working climate and generate greater commitment among the media men.

Organizations are man-managed and media personnel responsible for the same need to be specialists in their disciplines. Professional competence, highly integrated personality, knowledgeability about local values and culture, imagination and sense of projection, sense of role commitment, honesty, purpose of sincerity, moral courage and willingness to work with people, are some of the more important attributes for effective media men. These may be inculcated through training as well through "on the job" involvements. Media men have the onerous responsibility of planning and programming the media contents and selecting the appropriate technologies for making communication more effective for development. Media men at all levels in the decentralized media organizations, should be knowledgeable about the developmental goals and values that need to be created for a vibrant and changing Indian social structure.

If "consensus", "freedom", "participation", "social solidarity", "social justice" and "equity" are some of the developmental values to be promoted, then media men would prove counterproductive if they project values related to "Mandal", "Mandir", "Masjid", 'self-determination and separation' as these will result in spreading casteism, communalism, religious and ethnic violence, demand for a separate State, etc.; anti-developmental in nature and content.

In order to make development more ethno-oriented and decentralized, it would be desirable to allow the micro-economic organizations in the informal sector to grow and fill up the spaces left by the macro-economic structures of the nation-State. Their establishment at the micro-level can be instrumental in mobilizing men and money resources. They should not be considered a threat to macro-structures, instead they should be supported. At that level, development communication policy should foster political, economic and socio-cultural negotiations and integrations through various media of communication for arriving at consensus for the desired common values.

The micro social action groups or NGOs (non-governmental organizations) can play significant role in making development need-oriented, value-based and solidarity focused. Participation of people at micro level for decision-making on development initiatives can be energized by the "conscientization" process. As such, with regard to the development communication perspectives, it is the conscientization approach that needs to be given a priority. in our decentralized development planning. It is only through this perspective that the other perspectives of development communication such as development of empathy, diffusion and adoption of innovations and the magic multiplying effect of electronic media can have deeper penetration into the way of life of people.

Media from above represent information, whereas media from below and across represent communication. Media (culture) may be a reflection of our social structure but from development communication perspective, these have to be moulder of society through creation and presentation of new images of Man and his institutions. Let us, therefore, behold media to behold development.

Reference

Somavia, Juan, 1981, 'The Democratization of Communication: From Minority Social Monopoly to Majority Social Representation': *Development Dialogue*: 2.

10

Dynamics of Development in the Indian Society

Development is a dynamic concept of a stable society while economic growth and structural changes are its main expressed or implied goals. The stability of a society does not rule out. The existence of conflicts, tensions and fissions within a social system. In fact, these are there and for the system to acquire an orderly state, these need to be resolved, managed and fused by the institutional structures available to or reformulated by the society. Development has to be treated as an integral whole and as a cultural process taking note of natural environment, social relations, production, consumption and social well being of the people. It is the "people" who have to be the main elements of development and it is their preparation and activation that should be the cause and consequence of development. This may suggest that development should spring up from the heart of each society. In other words, each society should first rely on its own strength and sources for its people before it could think of moving outwards to other societies who may share its problems and aspirations (Mehta, 1984).

But the fast moving changes in the world economy during the last two decades or so, are not without significant effects on the development levels of the developing societies. The world economy has changed from being international to transnational which has no political boundaries and impinges significantly upon the domestic economies of the national states. It is the flow of money rather than the trade in goods and services that shapes the transnational economy and the economic politics of the sovereign national governments. They provide sharp reaction to the situations prevailing in the transnational money and capital markets. It is argued that in the transnational economy, the traditional factors of production, such as land and labour, and even money which is now universally available, have become secondary. Even the foreign exchange rates matter only for short span of time. It is management now that has become the decisive factor of production. As such, the economic policies of the sovereign national states get linked to and become dependent upon the regional economic powers, world economy of money, credit and investment. The organization and management of the same has been made possible by the information revolution and transnational enterprises. That would mean, newer transnational ecology and development of transnational laws to manage it (Drucker, 1989-90). Even the recent far reaching changes observed in the east European societies are indicative that they have failed to tackle their problems inwards and their economic compulsions have forced the political systems of their national states to advocate and adopt structural changes encouraging democratic forces to operate in the decision-making processes. However, it must be made clear that the macro economic development cannot tackle the micro economic problems of the developing nations.

Apart from market maximization encouraged by the transnational world economy, the mass media information flow has conscientized the people of these countries to new options and alternatives because of their raised aspirations, hopes and expectations. Neo-Marxists who have labelled ills of liberal societies to the path of capitalism seem to be now caught up by a dilemma of hope and despair because of the increasing, influence of transnational powerful capitalist economic order and the strong influence of mass communication channels across the national boundaries of different societies. The above challenges call for an alternative strategy or action for the development of the developing nations.

A team of researchers carried out an exercise in various countries of Latin America to suggest "an option for the future" in the form of "Human Scale Development". This was basically arrived at by analysing the human needs, scale and efficiency by focusing on unemployment and local development financing. It is primarily based on the dictum that the purpose of the economy is to serve the people and not the people to serve the economy and also on an indepth analysis of the nature of human needs. A new praxis based on Human Scale Development focuses on the satisfaction of fundamental human needs, on the generation of growing levels of self-reliance and on the construction of organic articulations of people with nature and technology, of planning with autonomy and of civil society with the state (Maxneef, *et. al.*, 1989).

Human needs, self-reliance and organic articulations are the foundations which support Human Scale Development. Further this strategy assumes a direct and participatory democracy. The basic postulate of Human Scale Development (HSD) is that development is about people and not about objects. It is considered inaccurate to view human needs as infinite, changing all the time and as different in each culture or environment as no effort is made to distinguish between needs and satisfiers of these needs. Instead, human needs must be understood as a system, interrelated and interactive. Except for the need of subsistence or to remain alive, no hierarchies exist within the system but the process of need satisfaction is often characterised by simultaneities, complementarties and trade offs. The human need structure has been classified along axiological needs such as the needs of *Subsistence, Protection, Affection, Understanding, Participation, Idleness, Creation, Identity and Freedom* and along existential needs, such as the needs of *Being, Having, Doing* and *Interacting*. These have been interacted to provide a matrix of needs and satisfiers (For example, in the classification provided, food and shelter are not to be viewed as needs but as satisfiers of the fundamental need for subsistence).

It is assumed that the fundamental human needs are the same in all cultures and in all historical periods. The changes observed over time and through cultures relate only to the ways or means by which the needs are satisfied. Unemployment and external debt are the two major problems of the Third World nations. It is through a set of satisfiers (destroyers, pseudo, inhibiting, singular and synergy) that the above problems of a given society are taken care of. These are not related to the available economic goods but to everything which, by virtue of representing focus on *Being, Having, Doing* and *Interacting*, contributes to the actualization of human needs.

The development options should move from the linear to the systemic approach and from efficiency to synergy. In other words, the human need structure and the associated roles and attributes of satisfiers should provide direction to the development strategy as well as there should be permanent stimulations for creating synergy satisfiers which satisfy a given need and at the same time stimulate and contribute to the fulfilment of other needs. This would usher participation of people and they would do the management of their needs through a self-reliant approach. Further, the invisible sectors or the micro organizations and their economic activities may fill the gaps or spaces left out by the macro organizations or formal economic structures and work towards increasing degree of self reliance for the transformation of economic and social relationships basic to the construction of a democratic culture, However, this should go along with the availability of resources necessary for generation of economic surpluses, thus, making way for the reproduction and growth of these organizations. The State, on the other hand, should not consider this invisible world as a threat to its macro organizational structures. Instead, the efforts should be to complement and supplement the role of the these micro organizations to have a sustainable, self-reliant and participatory development process through deconcentration and decentralization of political power (Maxneef et. al, 1989).

A democratic country like India has to look towards a perspective based on Human Scale Development for fulfilling the ideals of freedom, equality and social justice in developing its people.

Dynamics of Development: An Indian Experience

India adopted planned development nearly five decades ago. Mixed economy was adopted to function as a planning process in which the private sector was formally recognized along with the public sector but this was considered a transitional stage. Ultimately it was hoped that the private sector would be replaced by the public sector. Efforts were made to establish the fundamentals of a socialist structure and to fulfil the democratic principles laid down in our Constitution through Five-Year Plans (the First Five-Year Plan became effective in April, 1951) and community development programmes.

An examination of the planning process during the last five decades shows that although the initiators of planned development were inclined towards socialistic values like reduction of income disparities, equality and upliftment of the rural masses, yet in due course of time, it turned out to be lopsided in terms of income distribution. Despite planned efforts during these years, a greater proportion of people are poor. The path of mixed economy muddled through the development process and most of the decisions on economic issues and matters were influenced by private interests rather than by the Government. Further, economic progress became largely dependent on the development of the private sector. In order to determine the extent of private investments along with public investment for balanced economic growth, the State had to develop policies of inducements and restrictions. But due to the lack of coordination in government policies, the private sector was given an edge over public investments for industrial growth and agricultural development. This has resulted in increased disparity of consumption standards among the people. Further, there was a visible trend of income disparities over the years and an increased concentration of wealth and power in the hands of a small segment of the population. In addition, institutional measures like land reforms could not be successfully implemented.

Despite efforts to maintain consistency and uniformity in the approach to the mixed economy during the first three five-year plans, in reality the development process fell short of expectations. The growth and influence of the private sector over the years resulted in a plan holiday in March 1966, after the Third Five-Year Plan. This was a three-year planless period, the Fourth Five-Year Plan started only in April 1969. This plan period encouraged the private sector to further investment in certain important areas of economy like power, fertilizer and aluminium, which were reserved for public sector development according to industrial policy resolution of 1956. After the Fourth-Five Year Plan, in March 1974, the Fifth-Five Year Plan was launched but it was not allowed to run its course due to political and ideological changes at the national and state levels. This plan was abandoned a year before its period of completion. The Sixth Five-Year Plan was not allowed to take final shape and instead a time bound plan, a rolling plan to be renewed every year was suggested in order to adjust the targets. Though the public sector still received official support yet the private sector grew and expanded not only in infrastructural areas but also in largest profit making consumer goods and services. The subsequent Sixth and Seventh Five-Year Plans, claim to have lowered the percentage of people below the poverty line through special rural employment schemes. Again, the Eighth Five-Year Plan was reformulated due to political changes and the Ninth Five-Year Plan is also facing the same problem.

Apart from the increase in income disparities and concentration of wealth and economic power among the affluent classes in society, the Indian bourgeoisie got into league with international bourgeoisie, giving a startling fillip to the multinational corporations, the assets of which are reported to have increased by manifolds. Again, in the agricultural sector, the green revolution in the northern wheat growing areas of India has led to increasing disparities between the rural rich and the rural poor. In addition to being affluent, the rich landowners, over the years, have become a political force to be reckoned with. Some scholars argue that the economic crisis of today is due to disproportionate expansion of public expenditure to the overall production. There is an unwarranted alarming increase in the non-planned expenditure, which includes expenditure on defence and administration (Rabindra Nath, 1977). Increased investments by the private sector and decontrol of regulations on certain enterprises also resulted in generating a parallel economy and this further widened the gap between the haves and the have-nots.

It has been suggested that only after 1962, when resources began to be directed towards defence that the national economy started developing strains. The economy was further adversely affected after the 1971 war. It is further stated that the concentration of investments in the urban areas is benefitting a small segment of population whereas a vast majority of the population (75 per cent) living in the rural areas are deprived of resources. Even the investment in the agricultural sector has benefitted the large scale and rich farmers and the gap in the level of income and style of living is growing between the rich farmers and the landless labourers and marginal farmers. It cannot be said that planned efforts have not yielded dividends. Perhaps, in terms of physical targets, India's achievements are appreciable but the development process has been skewed. Unless the process is reversed, there is hardly any hope of fulfilling the socialist values.

Although India started with a 'bottom up' approach to planning, this was soon converted to 'top-down' multilevel planning. During the Third Five-Year Plan, grass-root planning was envisaged but the 'district' and 'block' plans could not become feasible or viable. The district plans remained a bundle of isolated, ad hoc schemes prepared by various state departments. Most of these programmes launched through the five-year plans lacked flexibility. The programmes were uniformally structured throughout the country although different regions required special methods or approaches. Further, there was a lack of integration at the local level due to inadequate and faulty coordination. Factors like the spatial organization of settlements in terms of providing efficient facilities and services and the need for human resource development was not given due attention. Even the planning for rural areas was devoid of its functional link with the urban centres.

Further, the Five-Year Plans were basically economic plans stressing economic growth in terms of industrial and agricultural output and did not focus on the social and cultural factors which were equally relevant to the total development process. Economic development and social change should be complementary processes. If the value system and social organization of the people is not changed, economic and technological advancements result in 'Cultural Lags' which are mainly responsible for maladjustments, tensions and disturbances. Of late, there has been a realization on the part of planners of the importance of social, cultural and political factors in the development process.

Various factors seem to have complicated the socialistic approach to the planned development over the last five decades. These factors include the vested interests of the national bourgeoisie which increased the role of the private sector in areas reserved for public undertakings, the war with China and the subsequent two wars with Pakistan putting great stress on the plan expenditure, the split of Congress Party in 1969 and subsequent shift of emphasis on the special area development programmes (CAD, SFDA, MFDA, DPAP, HADP, TDP, etc.), the declining importance of CD programmes, the failure of Panchayati Raj institutions in some areas and of these getting defunct in certain states, restricting democratic decentralization and devolution of power due to rigid compartmentalization between the bureaucratic structure and the development structure, elected legislators, parliament members and ministers, not willing to part with their leadership positions and encourage new leadership, reluctance on the part of bureaucrats to change their attitudes and give up their power functions to technocrats, the plan holiday, the ideological changes in planning, politicization of peasants, caste affiliations, concentration of wealth with the urban and rural rich, competition between the urban and rural rich to capture power positions in the state assemblies and Parliament, consciousness of the rural rich and their politicization to demand their rights vis-à-vis the urban rich and the reaction of the urban rich towards peasant movements, traditions and cultural ethos embedded in religious beliefs, philosophy and dogmas, belief in *Karma* and life after death, fatalism and destiny.

In addition to above, adhocism, inadequate information system to generate reliable data for planning, ignoring scientific techniques for planning and overreliance on value judgements, target oriented policies of administrators, time constraints to meet targets, apathy on the part of the rural poor, illiteracy, marginality, caste and class factors, social and economic rivalries and party politics, are some other factors which have resulted in marginal development of rural areas in our country.

Further, the designing of five-year plans has been centralised. The Planning Commission, in consultation with various ministries at the Centre, has remained the sole agency for determining national priorities and has been influenced by the national leadership or party in power. The different states have hardly any leeway to lay down their priorities. Although the various states have set up planning departments, they are actually looking after the utilization of resource allocation and their priorities are in keeping with national priorities. The situation at the district level is much more confusing. Though district plans were conceived of as a part of planned efforts within the guidelines provided by the State, their implementation could not become a reality in view of inadequate resources and political interests of certain legislators and ministers.

Some Indian Marxists suggest a cause-effect relationship between the capitalist path of development followed by national leaders in India and the problems of society, as reflected in the skewed development of the people. However, it may be a little too presumptuous to think so unless a casual relation between the two can be established. There could be some association between the two but the scale of economy can be reduced in terms of profit making. However, in the capitalist mode of development, it goes without saying that despite the introduction of socialistic patterns in economic growth and the reduction of profit-making, one cannot eliminate inequality completely. In addition to increasing the equality of income distribution, what is more important is decreasing the ascriptive basis of income distribution, that is, increasing the social mobility of the individual. But Marxists argue that a choice has to be made between these two priorities of equality and increased inequality (Benge, 1972). A choice, however, has also to be made between the value of freedom on the one hand and that of having the minimum need of food and shelter on the other hand. Suppression of one's freedom of thought, speech and action is likely to stunt the growth of the individual and one has to evaluate it along with the value of equality or inequality.

Irrespective of the fact of whether one follows on evolutionary or revolutionary path of development (a capitalist or non-capitalist path of development), in either case the development goals are influenced and shaped by dominant personalities who usually keep the path of development chequered and unclear. The goals set are invariably highly unrealistic and their accomplishments are illusionary. These are set purposely by such persons in order to keep themselves in dominant positions within the social system. When these people lose importance in the political scene, new ones take over and they ordain development goals and processes. Therefore, it appears to be psychological determinism which seems to interact with economic or ideological determinism while the value system and the social organization of a society are employed as instruments to relate development plans to the needs of the people. One cannot eliminate elites even in the revolutionary system of development as party elites assume privileges and benefits which keep their distinct from the common mass. Depending upon them rank and length of service in the party, they acquire a differential status. Thus, the stratification system or the system of inequality instead of operating on the vertical plane becomes functional on the horizontal plane. However, the biggest advantage is that the income disparities are reduced in this system.

However, the hallmark of India's struggle for freedom has been the principle of non-violence preached and practised by Mahatma Gandhi. The democratic ideals of Nehru pervaded the Indian scene and did not allow the more militants plans of other leaders to fructify and gain popularity among the masses. The people accepted Gandhi's and Nehru's ideals as these seemed more relevant to the Indian tradition of passivity, persuasion, persistence and self-control (Mehta, 1984).

Development Options for the Indian Society

Because of cultural or civilizational factors, India still has an opportunity for rural development within a democratic framework (Franda, 1979). The Indian tradition is characterized by a cultural ethos and a value system embedded in our religious philosophy and Hindu way of life (Modal value system). Some of the major values upheld in our society are conciliation or reconciliation, tolerance, sympathy, hierarchy, affection and warmth expressed through sentiments and emotions, belief in an Almighty God as a creator, preserver and destroyer of the universe, fructification of actions according to one's *Karma* or deeds, spirituality and belief in reincarnation, mutual help or cooperation, hospitality and concern for the needy and suffering. Although modernising influences have affected some of these values, yet in practice preference is given to these over values of conflict, intolerance, hostility, rudeness, rationality and reward according to one's efforts, self-orientation and materialism. Note that these values are non-existent in Indian society, but traditional values are still strongly upheld by a large segment of the population (Mehta, 1984).

Although India is the largest democracy in the world, yet democratic principles and ideals have not been allowed to function freely. Democratic principles need to be accelerated by educating individuals to make the right choices from the available alternatives. The planning process during the last five decades within the framework of democratic principles and ideals (as laid in the Constitution of India) failed to break down the social solidarity groups like caste and kinship. Instead, the ethnic identities became more pronounced than before due to lopsided development process.

A group of four scholars basing their observations on a case study "Bhoomi Sena: A Struggle for People's Power" in Maharashtra remarks that India as yet has not been able to establish and sustain an expanding cycle of accumulation and realization of surplus value, as such she is not a capitalist country but one moving towards capitalism with greater sense of direction and speed than most of the other developing nations. In other words, she has "oasis of capitalism in a precapitalist desert". In order that she frees herself from the trap of this precapitalist stagnation, she has to rely more on rural productive forces and with it the internal market than banking heavily on drives for foreign markets. The realization of this goal by the Indian bourgeoisie can be effected through (1) petty bourgeois elites of the urban area to live and integrate with the rural poor and lift them up through education, organization and the provision of technical expertise. However, this approach has proved ineffective. (2) Reliance on the emerging rural bourgeoisie to develop an agrarian capitalism. But the rural bourgeoisie is still a relatively weak class and one is doubtful whether they, on their own, can perform the major task of capitalist transformation of rural India. This would necessitate transfer of resources from urban to rural areas for building up both physical and social infrastructure necessary for capitalist growth. The question is whether urban bourgeoisie will allow such a massive mobilization of resources to rural areas or not. It has many other implications of political and social nature. (3) Dependence on an alliance between the two emerging rural classes capable of developing the productive forces, the bourgeoisie and the proletariat for the development of rural capitalism as has been experimented in Kerala and West Bengal. In other words, it has to be an efficient "communist" management of capitalism, that is, to mobilize both the proletariat and peasantry to develop the productive forces under capitalist relations of production, with a minimum cost to the bourgeoisie. (4) A class conscious rural proletariat who may start in certain areas the development of the productive forces under collectivist relations of productions (de Silva *et al*, 1979).

Whether it is development of rural capitalism or development of rural collectivism, one thing is certain that it is the "people" who have to set in the centre of development. There is a need to evolve systems which empower people and which release their capacities and give them incentives for change. Without these and without the deconcentration and decentralization of power, investment and technology have no meaning so far as development of the developing nations is concerned despite the influences of the transnational economy which has far reaching consequences. Rene Dubos, a French ecologist, proverbial expression states that "Think Globally but Act Locally". In the light of above, we have observed that centralized planning has resulted in creating dependency among the people. This has to be changed in order to develop self-reliance, which is basic to the development of people. It is only through the participation of the people in development activities that one can ensure their commitment to develop themselves as well as their community and to build up confidence in them to take decisions on their own. To realize all this a multidimensional paradigm focusing on institutional technological, infrastructural, participative and service oriented changes have been suggested to effect the village social structure in terms of occupational diversification, social mobility, reduction in income disparities, change in values and social relationship for an integrated living. This can be effected through decentralized planning and the consequent involvement and commitment of community leaders (Mehta, 1984).

For the development and welfare of people, Man and his institutions, Man and his tools and techniques, Man and his interests and Man and his justice should match and be compatible with needs, aspirations and motivations. The development effects in rural areas should be dynamic and fast changing and these changes are required to pace up with the fast changes occurring in urban areas. This would correspond well with the elements of the Human Scale Development and make development a participatory process within the democratic framework. It is observed that the developing nations, as a reaction to the centripetal forces of modernizing economy, have given rise to centrifugal forces, resulting in uprising and strengthening of ethnic and cultural identities. For sustainable social and cultural development, a wider representation of these groups in democratic set up is highly required to be taken up in future plan.

References

Benge, Ronald, (1972), *Communication and Identity*, London, Clive Bingley.

de Silva, G.V.S. *et. al*, (1979), "Bhoomi Sena: A Struggle for People's Power", *Development Dialogue*, 1979 : 2.

Drucker, Peter F, (1989), *The New Realities*, Professional Publishing, Oxford. Excerpt of the book "The World According to Drucker", in *Best of Business International*, Vol. 2, No. 1, Winter 1989-90, London, Whittle Communications International (U.K.) Limited.

Franda, Marcus, (1979), *Small is Politics : Organizational Alternatives in India's Rural, Development*, New Delhi, Wiley Eastern Ltd.

Maxneef, Manfred, *et., al*, (1989), "Human Scale Development : An Option for the Future", *Development Dialogue*, 1989 : 1.

Mehta, S.R., (1984), *Rural Development Policies and Programmes: A Sociological Perspective*, New Delhi, Sage Publications.

Nath, Rabindra, (1977), "The Strategy for Planning", *Yojana*, 21, 7, 1-14 May.

11

Backwardness, Population and Development

This chapter consists of four parts. In the first, the concept of backwardness will be conceived while in the second part, methodology to know the magnitude of backwardness along with operational indicators to determine it will be highlighted. In the third part, the socio-demographic consequences of backwardness will be analyzed while in the last, in the wake of backwardness, the possibility of India moving towards a Civil Society will be examined.

Concept of Backwardness

Backwardness has to be conceived in relation to forwardness. Backwardness implies a worse state directed to a rear or a starting-point and to the reluctance, shyness and dullness (of individuals or groups) whereas on the contrary, forwardness means moving onwards or towards the front, and advancement or progress (of individuals or groups) towards maturity or completion. (*Concise Oxford Dictionary*). In respect of human, these definitive notions need to be a converted into a construct comprehensive enough to include within its fold the socio-cultural, psychological, economic and political dimensions.

In order to understand backwardness in the sociological perspective, one has to start with the assumption that all men are born equal. This assumption was shared by Rousseau who thought that in a presocial original state, there was complete equality of all, that is, no one was considered to be superior to any one in rank or status. According to him, inequality came as a result of leaving the state of nature, and adopting the concept of property. The concept of property as a significant factor in creating inequality was also voiced by other scholars like Marx.

While Rousseau vouched for return to original state of nature for restoring equality among Men, Marx dreamt of a communist society for tackling the problem of inequality (Dahrendorf, 1969).

When we examine backwardness in the context of equality or inequality, it becomes clear that in the course of human growth and development, some Men have moved forward while others have lagged behind. This may be attributed to personal (individual) or social (societal) factors. At the individual level, there are natural differences observed in physical features, character, interests besides differences of rank in intelligence, talent and strength. On the other hand, at the societal level, there is social differentiation of positions essentially equal in rank and there is social stratification based on reputation and wealth expressed in terms of the rank order of a social status. In fact, in human development, it is the interaction of an individual with the society (institutions) that has resulted in the advancement of some more than that of others.

This interaction assumes polemics similar to that of influence of heredity and environment on Man's growth and development. Basically, it is the inequalities of intelligence, talents, character, interests, property, wealth, division of labour, social differentiation, occupational positions, rank ordering of activities according to their functional importance, social sanctions and norms that have resulted in backwardness or forwardness of human beings. Man has acquired, most of these characteristics, through various historical epochs. As such, inequality or backwardness is a historical phenomenon rather than inherited from one person to another as a biological one. In other words, backwardness is a socially constructed phenomenon and its solution also lies in providing social interventions.

Objective position of a group in terms of economic condition in the structure and the prevailing value system related to traditional position, occupation and lifestyle have been suggested as factors contributing to determining social backwardness (Shah, 1991). If we were to operationalize this conception, broadly we may discern income either generated through land or labour, caste status, caste linked occupation and standard of living as the major parameters for social backwardness of groups, although no reference, in the above concept is made with regard to the status of individuals.

No doubt, individuals constitute groups or are part of groups, but when one speaks of egalitarianism, the merit or the talent of an individual matters a lot in a society. It is also argued that certain claims made for a more just distribution of benefits and burdens on behalf of individuals are not identical with those made on behalf of groups. Further it is referred that despite far reaching changes in the institutional systems there is neither elimination nor reduction in income inequalities between individuals (Beteille, 1991).

The distinction between an individual and a group becomes even important from the point of view of social mobility of certain individuals within a group. Individual may improve their social status, but the groups to which they belong do not move up in the hierarchical social ladder. This raises another important issue as to what should be the unit of analysis while delineating social backwardness. Could it be an individual, group, community or a nation? Depending upon the unit of analysis, we shall have to conceive of the attributes or characteristics
that may conceptualize social backwardness for a given society. Further, we may have to think about the indicators that go along with measuring this social phenomenon. This will set limit to the general conceptualization of backwardness. However, an attempt can be made to identify the critical variables, interconnected and interrelated in such a manner so as to provide comprehensive understanding of this concept.

Backwardness cannot be delinked from the poverty conditions of living as the majority of the backward classes or groups are either poor or ultra poor. Poverty has been defined in terms of both absolute and relative dimensions. (The "absolute poor" have been defined as those having income per person too low to afford 2250 calories per person per day and susceptible to poverty induced undernutrition). Apart from income and nutritional levels, structures related to asset ownership affect the proportions of persons that are non-poor, poor or ultra poor. It is observed that in India, 10-20 per cent of people who constitute the ultra poor or the poorest are different than the further 25-35 per cent who fall below the 2250 calorie live. (Lipton, 1988). Even, they are differentiated on the basis of food intakes, health hazards and labour productivity. Besides strong economic connotation of poverty, scholars have now started speaking of several kinds of poverties (Maxneef et. al, 1989).

In other words, apart from economic deprivation, poverty needs to be conceived in terms of social, cultural, psychological and political deprivations as this set limits to the poor sharing status, values, recognition and participation in development of activities with the non-poor. As such, we may conceive a poor as a person who is not only deprived of his purchasing power to buy food enough for him or for the existence of the members of his family but one who is also alienated socio-culturally and psychologically to the extent that he is discriminated against in his own group, community or nation. Poverty, on the other hand, may be conceived as a phenomenon isolating certain persons in the population to the extent of depriving them of their status or position in the society because socio-structural, cultural and politico-economic factors (Mehta, 1988).

If we apply the extensions of the concept of poverty to that of backwardness, apart from the social, cultural, psychological and political dimensions, economic standing and nutritional level stem out as outstanding variables for delineating the backwardness of an individual, group or a community. The democratic system has allowed persons from different strata of population to have political participation through adult franchise. Further, in a stratified society like India, due to new complexes of institutionalization, industrialization, trade and commerce, expansion of means of communication, migrations, technology, exposure to mass media and widespread of education and health services, many individuals within different social groups both in rural and urban areas, have moved up in the social hierarchy. This has led to the emergence of a middle class and many individuals from the backward groups especially go-getters entered into it acquiring a new social status. Despite a large correspondence between the caste and occupation in the traditional sense there is a new class status as a result of the occupational differentiation process. Thus social status in terms of caste or class becomes another important variable for determining backwardness of an individual or a community. This will be largely reflected by the occupational position of an individual in the social structure.

To a large extent, the social mobility of individuals could be possible because of increased social and psychological capacities of persons or group of persons. Thus, lack of education or information will influence the personality development of persons and they may tend to become submissive, alienated, lehargic and fatalist. Poor health condition of their living can further deteriorate their productivity. This can be ascertained mainly through the location of residence of the people. Overcrowded dwellings, insanitary living conditions and non-disposal of refuge may reflect their living environment indicative of their backwardness. Another important dimension of backwardness among Indians (especially among the Hindus) is the value orientation embedded in the framework of Karma (past action or deeds) and Dharma (that which is right and moral). This has generated more deeply among the persons in the lower caste groups than those in the upper strata. As a result of their faith in Karma theory, many have developed apathy, lethargy, lack of inertia and fatalism while they may lack values such as openness to new ideas, scientific outlook and future orientation, necessary for their progress or advancement.

Thus, backwardness may be conceived in terms of economic standing (income, wage or landholding status) nutritional level, social status in terms of caste or class, educational attainment, healthful living environment and value orientations of persons or group of persons. These have to be evaluated in relation to forward categories, depending upon the unit of analysis, in question. However, these six fold dimensions of backwardness are not mutually exclusive.

Magnitude and Indicators of Backwardness

After an attempt at delineation of backwardness, it shall be worthwhile to identify the magnitude of this social phenomenon. If poverty has a bearing on backwardness then poverty in the Indian setting was estimated to be 80 per cent in 1861 while in 1947, at the dawn of independence, 60 per cent people were reported to be below the poverty line. (Punit, 1982). During the last nearly five decades, governmental efforts through poverty alleviation programmes, and more rapid growth measures, have led to a rise in the agricultural wages and in the consumption levels of people at the lower end of the income distribution during 1970s and also in first half of the 1980s. This has resulted in reduction in the prevalence rate of poverty. Various estimates suggest that as many as 40 per cent of the population in India may have income below the poverty line (The World Bank, 1989). The official figures put up by the Government consider 37 per cent of the population in the country as below the poverty line. However, the World Development Report (1990) provides a grim picture of India's economy since it is estimated that India's growth is unlikely to exceed two per cent per capita a year over the next decade. If the economic growth average is maintained at 5 per cent and per capita GDP (Gross Domestic Product) at 3 per cent, the poverty count in India by 2000 the next year would be 370 millions as against 255 millions. A rise in the absolute number of poor in the country will have a depressing effect on backwardness.

Apart from the 40 per cent people in the absolute poverty group, there may be another 10-15 per cent of people in the relative poverty group (persons having an annual income less than one-third of the national average). This may put the magnitude of poor in the country to about 55 per cent. They are spread out in different communities located at various geographical and cultural regions of the country. Sociologically speaking, they may also be referred as backward and underprivileged as they do not have a normal standard of living or rights in the community because of their weak social and economic status, political subjugation and religious fatalism. These backward or underprivileged communities in India can be currently grouped as (1) Scheduled Tribes (2) Scheduled Castes and (3) other Backward communities (Women, Children, people in urban slums, physically and mentally retarded persons are other underprivileged groups in our society).

Of the 4635 communities (based on People of India Report, Anthropological Survey of India) as many as 400 (they constitute 8.0 per cent of the total population, Census 1991) tribal groups are spread over the different regions of the country. On the other hand, there are as many as 1108 Scheduled Caste groups constituting 16.4 per cent of the total population of the country (Census 1991). Together, they constitute nearly 25.0 per cent of our population. The other backward communities include (a) nomads who have taken to begging, mimicry, jugglery, dancing etc.; (b) landless labourers, (c) tenants without occupancy rights/insecure land tenures (d) small landowners with uneconomic holdings (e) artisan and occupational classes without security of employment as traditional occupations have ceased to be remunerative and (f) communities without sufficient education and representation in government services. (GO1, 1955).

According to Mandal Commission appointed by the Government of India in 1978 to look into the problems of OBCs and suggest redressal measures, they have been estimated to be 52 per cent of the total population of the country. This was arrived at by analyzing the caste distribution data of 1931 Census, and on the basis of a sample survey of two villages and an urban block in each district of the country. Four social, three educational and four economic indicators respectively were employed for determining caste backwardness. Using educational level (up to primary either father or grandfather) and income level (consumption level of Rs. 71 per head per month at 1971 prices) of the people and on the basis of differential score weightage for these indicators, Mandal Commission arrived at the total population of OBCs. (GO1, 1980). This rough methodology has been questioned by some scholars (Sharma, 1990).

If we were to go by caste composition of the country, roughly not more than 10 per cent of the twice born castes may constitute our population whereas nearly 30 per cent may constitute the Scheduled Castes and Tribes, the remaining population (say about 60 per cent) may constitute the backward classes or middle castes. The domination of these 10 per cent of the higher castes in the social, economic and political life has compelled the backward communities to launch protest movements in the different parts of the country. As a consequence, they secured preferential treatment for them so far as their admissions to educational institutions, and entry to legislative assemblies, parliament and government departments are concerned. (Our constitution has already provided reservations to STs and SCs (23 per cent of total population) for admission to educational institutions and government services, but this reservation was also sought by the backward communities as well)..

Although the Mandal Commission had recommended reservations for OBCs in educational institutions and government service, the report was pending with the Congress regimes of Indira Gandhi and Rajiv Gandhi, as in certain quarters, it was believed that a further reservation of 27 per cent, (This figure of 27 per cent is set because of the ceiling of reservation put forth by the Supreme Court of India. As per legal code, the total reservation cannot exceed beyond 50 per cent of our population) in addition to already 23 per cent given to SCs and STs, may tantamount to ignoring the merit, efficiency and talents in the country. However it was during Janta Dal's regime, that V.P. Singh became the champion of OBCs when he announced 27 per cent reservations for them in educational institutions and government service. (Some of the government service sectors such as Scientific institutions and organizations and Defence services were excluded from the composition of this reservation.)

This announcement of V.P. Singh was a frustrated bid to stick to the power but this was met with a sharp reaction from the upper caste Hindus especially in the northern States; (southern States as well as the States in the west had already a long history of reservation policy for OBCs). Its manifestation was marked by protest movements, firing and self-immolation of youth on a large scale that was never observed in the post independent India. Merit, talent and efficiency of an individual were sidetracked. However, the protest movement was so strong and widespread that it resulted in the debacle of V.P. Singh ministry. The matter was referred to the Supreme Court. As per the constitutional requirement of the country, the government was committed to provide preferential treatment to the disadvantaged groups as a requisite of equality especially to Scheduled Castes, Scheduled Tribes, Other Backward Classes, women and children (Katzanstein, 1983).

P.V. Narasimha Rao's government (Congress Party) voucned for economic criterion to be added along with caste based classification of OBCs. However, the Supreme Court upheld the reservation policy of government (27 per cent) for OBCs in government services with a rider that those who have moved up in the ladder of social hierarchy due to mobility and constitute a creamy layer among the OBCs, will be denied this concession of reservation. V.P. Singh, again tried to voice for OBCs as he was challenging the criteria of government, (that is those having 60 per cent of the irrigated landholdings of the land ceiling of 18 acres and having a family member holding a class II position in the government service) to constitute the creamy layer among the OBCs as he felt that these were inadequate for including persons in the creamy layer of OBCs. Notwithstanding the polemic nature of merit, talent, excellence and efficiency of individuals and reservation policy of certain groups in a democratic country, the magnitude of problem of backwardness is significant. This needs to be tackled to bring about at least equality of opportunities and access to resources, if not equality in absolute terms, through social engineering mechanisms.

As regards indicators of backwardness, these need to be based on the six dimensions delineated in the above respect. However, these have to be constructed while keeping in view the local cultural and regional imperatives and different states can evolve their own indicators of backwardness within the framework provided. Some of the broad indicators in respect of economic standing, nutritional level, social status, educational attainment, healthful living environment to determine backwardness may be land ownership status (no land, irrigated and unirrigated land), salaried and wage earners as per cent of total economically active population, adult male labour in agriculture as per cent of total adult male labour; professional, technical and related workers as per cent of total economically active population, apparent consumption of protein of animal origin per capita per day, different or same occupation of a son as that of father within a household, literate as per cent of total population of 15 years and over; expectation of life at birth, water supply and refuge disposal facilities, per cent of population with reasonable access to these facilities.

As regards value orientation of persons because of softness of data, more analytical-cum-descriptive indicators may be employed to classify persons with less appropriate actions from those with more appropriate actions on development initiatives. The cut off point for backwardness will have to be arrived at after assigning total scores on above indicators to each household in selected rural and urban areas. This may provide somewhat better account of the magnitude of backwardness in the country than attempted at by the Mandal Commission.

Population : Socio-Demographical Consequences of Backwardness

The massive absolute number of poor in our country is putting pressure or the fragile natural resource base, generating higher levels of landlessness and unemployment. It is reported that of the poorest one-fifth of households in the developing countries, between 55 and 80 per cent households have as many as eight or more members. (Lipton, 1988). As such, poverty or backwardness for that matter, because of low literacy level especially among females encourages early marriage, higher fertility, large family size, age specific mortality (especially more among females than males) infant mortality, child mortality and massive-migration from the household (especially from rural to urban areas) affecting the household size and composition. Thus the households belonging to backward communities remain big and young (more number of children), with high mortality and fertility as compared to the households of the forward communities. Further, the dependency ratio of persons in the backward households is likely to be more as children and old persons would depend more on the household earnings than on their investments and subsequent return on the investments.

Population growth at a higher rate among the backward communities is going to increase their problems of development. A greater number of children would need to be provided with education, nutritious food and health care. Further, there would be an increase in the number of people seeking jobs. This would need an increase in productive jobs. In order this to happen, the investments should grow faster than the labour force. But this is unlikely in a poor country as such there is bound to be a rapid growth of unemployment and underemployment. Due to low wage earnings, the poor individual families may not be able to afford to buy food they need, even if the natural food production may cope up with national population growth. The result would be an increase in the number of people living in "absolute poverty" that is conditions of life characterized by malnutrition, illiteracy and disease, much below any reasonable human decency. Pushing cultivation into hill sides, semi arid zones and tropical forests, in the absence of farmland, has further resulted in soil erosion. In addition, the demand for fire wood by the backward communities is increasing and the scarcity of the same is the main reason for deforestation (Ford Foundation, 1985).

Population growth has also resulted in widening income gaps between the backward and forward communities. In short, a fairly high fertility and moderate mortality makes the social well being of backward people more depressing because of low per capita income, high incidence of poverty and illiteracy especially among the females. Limited social mobility, lack of opportunities and lack of access to resources discourage a majority of backward communities to participate actively in the development initiatives and they tend to retrench themselves into their religious, linguistic and cultural ethnocentric ethnic groups. These ethnic formations and identities are susceptible to political mobilization and become vote banks for the politicians in a democratic system.

Development: Can India Move Towards a Civil Society?

According to Jaffery, social theory tends to consider a good society as one without strains and disruptions. Conservative thought suggests some kind of neo-traditional social and cultural integration for the restoration of social tranquillity while holding modernity responsible for tension in a society. On the other hand, radical theory blames capitalism and proposes socialism as an antidote to social disruption or strife. But both these theories are far from reality as every kind of society will produce some tension and crisis. In fact, the more that a Civil Society gets institutionalized the more do scandals, affairs and crisis become facts of social life. The main issue is not whether such tensions are created but how they are resolved to maintain the integrity and continuity of the civil society (Jaffery, 1990).

India is a democratic country and its aim is to attain a civil society. But, as a developing country, she has yet to acquire the basic expressions of a democracy such as lack of exploitation, equalization, generalized popular participation, the dignity of employment, adequate income, individual and social creativity (Somavia, 1981). However in its preamble, the Constitution of India has laid down social justice, equality and fraternity as basic goals to be accomplished through democratic means.

Political systems committed to democracy are seeking various combination of political, social, economic, and cultural democracy but in reality, they do not have a satisfactory arrangement. Perhaps, there is a need for a shift in the social science theories studying democratic societies. Instead of having myopically centred theories on social structure, we need to evolve a theory which is less structural and focuses on solidarity and social values, that is to what and how people speak, think and feel about politics. In other words, apart from considering political arrangements and narrowly defined institutional structures on the specific patterns of sanctions and rewards (separation of powers, legal rights and procedural guarantees and voting regulations) that prevent the abuse of power and rule by the few, there is also a need to include in this theory a complex network of supportive social arrangements that make democracy a dynamic process (Jaffery, 1990).

These social arrangements are beyond the structures of economic equality so often voiced in the materialist sense but they are indicative of social solidarity in universalistic terms, that is, in terms of weness of a national community, transcending particular commitments, loyalties and interests to forge a single thread of identity among the disparate people. It implies community of society, the Gesellschaft as a Gemeinschaft having collective consciousness and universal ties appealing to "impersonal" and highly generalized issues like rights and peoplehood. This community is to be defined as a collective of individuals each of whom is conceived as holding independent rights. Thus Civil Society is a dimension of a social organization that is rooted simultaneously in a radical individualization and a thorough collectivism. The mechanism by which the civil society, that is the solidarity representing the people of individuals regulates the struggle for power and interest is law ramified through enactment of "Constitution". Thus legal codes, Constitution, institution of "office", symbolic code or language articulating universalistic ties, cultural codes to represent people's expectations, denial to a particular person, or group an absolute right to power, and reinforcement of universalistic regulation that the "office" and the Constitution provide, are some of the main mechanisms that will provide framework to the power elites to function in a pluralized manner and move the people towards a civil society. These are ideals and perhaps, it is impossible to create a universal brotherhood of society itself. We may move only towards a restricted sphere of civil society. Neither capitalism nor socialism can eliminate the competition for scarce resources that are part of the organized social system and every struggle for scarce resources is bound to lead to instrumental and anti-normative dimensions. Even the struggle by elites for power and interest cannot be eliminated as that would depend upon the convergence or disconvergence of their interests with the people at large. These dangers to civil society need to be examined in respect of every nation State (Jaffery, 1990).

After having outlined the ideals and the mechanisms to achieve such ideals of a civil society given by Jaffery, it may be worthwhile to examine the extent to which Indian society could move towards it in the post independent democratic set up. Independent India got in legacy from the British, an economically and socially backward, exploited, discriminated and oppressed population, the majority of whom were living in conditions of abject poverty, malnutrition and insanitation. These backward communities were to be brought forward as a part of national goals of progress, advancement and social well-being through democratic means. This was a stupendous task and the national leadership of Congress party in governance then, framed a Constitution which stressed on equality, social justice and fraternity among the people through liberal means. Appropriate legal codes were formulated and the laws enacted by parliament were enforced by judiciary through executive institutions for the transformation of Indian society and for establishing an equal and just social order.

Over the years, the institutional structures established by the government have multiplied manifolds and these institutions are being given more importance over an individual. That denies an individual, his or her right to work and live comfortably. The process needs to be reversed and an institution should serve the individual rather than an individual serving the institution if equality of opportunities and social justice are to be promoted to improve the conditions of backward communities.

Through governmentalization and politicization, the institutional structures evolved rules and regulations that did not allow many to acquire their rights and exercise their wills. Notwithstanding the legal constraints, Indian democracy through development planning raised agricultural growth and industrial output. The service sector also got expanded. These economic measures over the last five decades or so led to a record agricultural production, extensive industrialization and consequent urbanization, social mobility of individuals due to economic differentiation processes leading to occupational diversification and scientific and technological advancement. Further, there has been expansion of education, health care and preferential treatment given to weaker sections of the society especially STs, SCs, OBCs, women and children to protect them from exploitation, discrimination and oppression that they have to face from the forward communities, in order to provide social justice, and promote equality and brotherhood among the people. But the development process remained lopsided as it created more income and consumption disparities between individuals, communities and regions. We started living in two worlds, the world of the rich and that of the poor. However, in this process of development, there has been an emergence of middle peasantry in rural India while that of middle class of traders and industrial entrepreneurs in urban areas besides some people entering into service sector from the backward communities because of reservation policy for them (The historical analysis and the merits and demerits of reservation policy have been discussed by other scholars, Beteillé, 1991; Shah 1991; Katzanstein, 1983; Sharma, 1990).

But due to population rise among the backward communities, the number of poor has been on increase and despite reservation policy for them in education, service and election, their condition of living has not changed objectively. In short, the developmental process under parliamentary democracy, well thought Constitution and well framed legal codes resulted in creating islands of wealth in the ocean of poverty and backwardness. It is observed that economic poverty reflects political poverty as the poor do not have means such as capital or trade union power for voicing their demands (Cardoso and Helwege, 1992). As such, the political system must generate economic activities for the backward and poor people so that they become active partners with others in the development initiatives.

Unfortunately, over the last few decades, the political system within the democratic framework in this country, starting with a socialistic slant acquired capitalistic overtones and presently has degenerated itself to the dubious forms of commercialization and criminalization. A host of scandals, affairs and crisis have appeared on the national scene. Some of the social and economic failures of the democratic political system observed in India relate to child labour, child marriage, discrimination against women, exploitation, discrimination and oppression of employees by the employers, separatist tendencies due to ethno-linguistic demands, communalism, untouchability, dowry disinformation, proxy wars, terrorism and militancy, Bofors gun deal, multicrore securities scam, and pay off to the Prime Minister for party elections. Besides, we have Shahbano case, demolition of Masjid and symbolic construction of Ram Temple at Ayodhya, protests against reservation policy for OBCs, water disputes between states, demand for a separate state (Gorkhaland, Jharkhand, Kashmir, etc.), demand for the impeachment of Chief Justice of India, postponement of elections by the Chief Election Commissioner, in a bid to override Parliament and the Supreme Court, and violation of anti-defection law, as some of the examples that adversely affect the legal codes and generate constitutional crisis.

In addition to above, despite Hindi being a link language as a part of three-language formula adopted in the country, linguistic ethnocentrism has weakened the process of having universalistic ties so necessary for a civil society. The development process, further raised the hopes and aspirations of people especially from the backward communities but the plans failed to relate their activities to the expected cultural code of the large majority. This resulted into frustration on the part of many who behaved either aggressively or regressively. As a consequence, we have a bouts of riots, bomb explosions, violence and strikes creating more chaos than order in the society. Our democratic system has failed miserably in curbing the vested interests of the power elites. They have actually refused to vacate their power positions for others and that has bred corruption and nepotism leading to a worst order in our social system. In fact, their motives of not functioning in a pluralized way has led to leadership crisis even among the backward communities.

As pointed out earlier, a democratic system is bound to generate strifes, disruptions and tensions within a social system. We have observed that the ideals of the civil society and the mechanisms to accomplish these have played feebly and inadequately in our society. These have generated tensions that need containment so as to avoid an anarchic state in our country. Further, we should allow the forward communities to cooperate with the backward communities for moving towards a civil society. In order to accomplish this ideal, what should be done to resolve the tensions and strifes that have arisen due to interaction of modern democratic institutional structures with the traditional value based Indian culture?

As a practitioner of sociology for long, I would venture to suggest a "People Centred" theory and practice to alleviate the lot of the poor and the backward people of this country. Growth of assets alone may not reduce economic poverty but the distribution of economic growth is a more plausible solution to the reduction of economic poverty in developing nations. Using data for 35 developing nations, Field, (1989) suggests that economic growth generally but not always reduce poverty. But the capitalist growth models in Indian setting have increased income disparities in different groups and regions. Despite technological breakthrough and its transfer to our country the trickle down effect of economy is limited and it has touched the problem of poverty and backwardness in a peripheral manner. Again, the present liberalized market economic measures adopted by the government may not act as a panacea for the eradication of poverty as with privatization on the move, the multinationals and the local industrial and commercial houses will look forward to recruit individuals having excellence, talent and merit. This will further marginalize the poor and the backward in our society. Suitable employment schemes will have to be envisaged for such marginalized groups so as to raise their purchasing power. Reservation policy for such groups may not help them to get out of the condition of drudgery. Social arrangements related to land management and industry shall also have to be altered in favour of such groups. In the wake of privatization, the private sector may be persuaded to accept the concept of trusteeship given by Gandhiji. This may establish new kind of values fostering cooperation and mutual trust between the rich and the poor.

As stated earlier, reduction in economic poverty is going to reduce political poverty and more and more people from the poverty groups will start making demands on the political system. This will enforce the political system to be more responsive and accountable to people from the different strata of the society. Wider participation of backward communities in the political process and deconcentration and decentralization of the power structures will reduce the dominance of power elites to retain their power positions. The political system will become largely pluralized. Electoral reforms to weed out corrupt and sharp practices in the election system at different levels of political process also need to be enforced for holding free and fair elections. Besides, with the introduction of 80th amendment bill (separation of religion from politics), there is a need to revise the Constitution. Market economy on the one hand, and the social welfare measures for the backward communities on the other hand, would throw up contradictions which may not be resolved through democratic process. If the Constitution is to be responsive to the poor and the backward classes in the country, it needs to look afresh at the issues as the socialistic slant advocated in the early years of independence may get diluted by the present market economic forces. The changed socio-economic scenario also calls for reformulation of legal codes to favour the backward communities, women and children in order to save them from exploitation, discrimination and oppression so often practiced in our society. The emerging cultural code reflecting the hopes, aspirations and needs of these people must be taken into account while revising Constitution and framing new legal codes.

Social relations are important in human development. An analysis of 51 poor countries showed that those countries whose citizens enjoyed greater political and civil liberties also experienced large improvements in life expectancy at birth, real income per head and infant survival rates (Das Gupta and Weale, 1992). The World Development Report (1990) also suggests that for reducing poverty, apart from creating income-earning opportunities through labour intensive technology, there is a need to strengthen social services such as education and health to increase the poor's capacity to respond to new opportunities. The most important characteristic of the poor that need a change for removing poverty is education, not only in formal sense but also in terms of skills. Primary education is an important means for raising productivity and hence growth. This holds good for improvement in health and nutrition. Data estimation for 88 developing countries by Wheeler (1980) and Morris (1982) indicate a significant impact on growth rates from increases in caloric intake and literacy rates. Morris study found that primary education enrollments showed favourable effect on growth rates of per capita income. More efficient allocation of government revenue, that is, its redistribution and that of foreign aid, are critical to elimination of poverty in developing nations (Cardoso and Helwege, 1992). In our context besides expansion of health care and education, population especially among the poor will not help them overcome their bad conditions of living.

The effective utilization of social services by the poor and the backward will also help them to respond to new occupational opportunities generated by the economic system and they may show an upward social mobility. This may help in improving the social status of individuals from the backward groups and this may, at the same time, weaken the caste and kinship solidarities. But the caste biases and prejudices against the backward communities are so entrenched in the minds of the forward communities that these need to be eliminated through greater interaction between the two communities, education, mass media exposure and interparticipation in religious and cultural fairs and festivals. These changes in social relationships will give rise to popular democracy and the political system will take note of what people feel and think about the democratic system.

The Indian tradition is characterized by cultural ethos and value system embedded in our religious and Hindu way of life (modal value). Some of the major values upheld in our society are conciliation, tolerance, sympathy, hierarchy, affection and warmth expressed through sentiments and emotions, belief in Almighty God as a creator, preserver and destroyer of the universe, spirituality and belief in reincarnation, mutual help and cooperation, hospitality and concern for the needy and suffering (Mehta, 1984). Some of these values are basics to establishment of Community as Society or Gesselschaft as Gemeinschaft and these can be fostered in our set up to move us towards a Civil Society. But over the years, the modernizing influences have thrown up values such as competition, jealousy, individualism, hatred, conflict, rudeness, rationality, reward according to one's efforts, self-orientation and materialism. Some of these values will have to be curbed and values such as unity, cooperation, frugality, humane and equitable conditions of living, will have to be reinforced among the people.

Despite linguistic ethnocentrism, as many as 325 languages based on People of India Report, Anthropological Survey of India, are spoken in this country, a unifying language, the language of Indian culture will have to be evolved. That should transcend the physical boundaries or regions, groups and communities and provide negotiated understandings and meanings about Indians across India. Perhaps the link language (Hindi) could be an effective medium in this direction. There is a need to develop people without disturbing their local language, knowledge and culture.

To conclude, no doubt the past is important for the present and the present is necessary for the future. But my contention is that national leadership instead of exciting people (especially the poor and the backward classes) about the past, should analyze the contemporary problems related to the development of the poor and the backward classes and show commitment and exercise will to tackle these on a well-informed basis. If our national leadership fails to live in the present, our future is going to be bleak and we, instead of moving towards a Civil Society, will be badly caught up in a web of barbarism. Moral should prevail over material, and the national leadership should opt for wider representation of backward communities within a democratic framework, eliminate ethnic discrimination, promote democracy, avoid two tiered economy of the rich and the poor, preserve local culture and encourage local participation through mass media openings, in addition to expansion of education, strengthening of health care services and curbing of population growth especially among the weaker sections of the society. Perhaps, with these measures there is some hope of moving towards a Civil Society. Only the national leadership has to improve its political will to implement these measures.

References

Beteillé, Andre, (1991), "Distributive Justice and Institutional well-being", *Economic and Political Weekly,* Vol. XXVI, Nos. 11 and 12 (Annual Number), Bombay. Sameeksha Trust Publications.

Cardoso, E. and A. Helwege, (1992), "Below the Line, Poverty in Latin America", *World Development,* Vol. 20, No. 1. (January).

Dahrendorf, Ralp, (1969), "On the origin of inequality among Men", *Social Inequality,* (ed), Andre Beteillé, London, Penguin Books.

Das Gupta, Partha and Martin Weale, (1992), "On Measuring the Quality of Life, "*World Development,* Vol. 20, No. I. (January).

Field, Gary, (1989), "Changes in Poverty and Inequality in Developing Countries", *The World Bank Research Observer,* Vol. 4, No. 2, quoted in Cardoso and Helwege, *op. cit.*.

Ford Foundation, (1985), *The Ford Foundation's Work in Population,* New York, (August).

Government of India, (1955), *Report of the Backward Classes Commission,* Vol. I, New Delhi.

Government of India, (1980), *Report of Backward Classes Commission (Mandal Commission),* New Delhi, Controller of Publications.

Jaffery, Alexander, (1990), "Democracy and Civil Society," (Draft Chapter), in his *Watergate and the Discourse of Civil Society,* Department of Sociology, Los Angeles, University of California.

Katzanstein, Mary Fanisod, (1983), "Preferential Policies, the Courts, and National Unity in India", *National Unity, the South Asian Experience,* (ed), Israel Milton, New Delhi, Promilla and Co.

Publishers.

Lipton, Michael, (1988), *"The Poor and the Poorest: Some Interim Findings,* (Discussion Paper), The World Bank Washington D.C.

Maxneef, Manfred, et. al., (1989), "Human Scale Development: An option for the Future", *Development Dialogue, 1.*

Mehta, S.R., (1984), *Rural Development Policies and Programmes: A Sociological Perspective,* New Delhi, Sage Publications.

Mehta, S.R., (1988), "Social, Structural and Cultural Dimensions of Rural Poverty", *Relevant Sociology,* Vol. V., No. 112.

Morris, Robin, (1982), *Economic Growth in Cross Section",* Mimeo (Washington D.C. World Bank) as quoted in Cardoso and Helwege, *op. cit.*

Punit, A.E., (1982), *Profiles of Poverty in India,* Delhi, B.R. Publishing Corporation.

Samavia, Juan, (1981), "The Democratization of Communication: From Minority Social Monopoly to Majority Social Representation", *Development Dialogue,* 2.

Shah, Ghanshyam, (1991), "Social Backwardness and Politics of Reservations", *Economic and Political Weekly,* Vol. XXVI, Nos. 11; 12 (annual number), Bombay, Sameeksha Trust Publications.

Sharma, S.L., (1990), "A dubious means of uplift", Chandigarh, *Indian Express,* October, 16.

Wheeler, David, (1980), *Human Resource Development and Economic Growth in Developing Countries: A Simultaneous Model,* World Bank Staff working paper (World Bank, Washington D.C.) as quoted in Cardoso and Helwege, *op. cit.*

World Bank, (1989), *India: Poverty, Employment and Social Services* (A country report), Washington D.C.

World Development Report, (1990), Published for the World Bank by the N.Y., Oxford University Press.

12

Dynamics of Sustainable Development in the Indian Society

India: A Profile

India, who rides a peacock, is a country of continental size. She is nourished richly by her cultural traditions and history. Her geographical size is gigantic (3.29 million square kilometres) while her population as per the 1991 Census is 846.3 million including the projected population of 7.72 million of Jammu and Kashmir. (Today, we are around one billion). She is the second most populous country in the world. Although, the country accounts only for 2.4 per cent of the total world area, yet she has 16 per cent of the population of world inhabiting her land. The sex ratio (number of females per 1,000 males) declined from 934 in 1981 to 927 in 1991 (excluding Assam and J&K). There has been slight increase in urban population, 26 per cent of the people live in urban centres. According to Sample Registration System (SRS) for 1991, 36 per cent of population consist of children (age 0-14 years), and 8 per cent elders (age 65 years and above). The average annual exponential growth rate has decreased from 2.22 per cent to 2.11 per cent (from 1971-81 to 1981-91 period). The national goal is to reach a net reproduction rate of 1.0 by 2011-2016. SRS estimates for 1992, shows a crude birth rate of 29.0 per 1000 population while the crude death rate is 10.0 per population. However, the infant mortality rate is 79 per 1000 live births. The Total Fertility Rate (TFR) is estimated to be 3.6 children per woman for 1991, while the Government of India's figure for couple protection rate (defined as percentage of eligible couple protected effectively against pregnancy) for 1992 is 44 per cent (National Family Health Survey, 1994).

According to 1991 Census, the literacy rate in India for people between the age of 7 years and above is 52 per cent (64 per cent for males and 36 per cent for females), while the life expectancy is 57 years. Population density per square kilometre of agricultural land is 41.5. The estimate is that population will cross one thousand million mark (1,002) by next year. while the same may get stabilized at 1,700 million mark. The per capita supply of calories per day is 2126 while the GNP per capita is about US $300. Only 80 per cent population in urban areas and 47 per cent in rural areas have access to safe drinking water. Labour participation rate for males is 39 per cent while for females, it is 55 per cent (the overall female labour force is 26 per cent of which 70 per cent are in agriculture and 13 per cent in industry). The age dependency is 77.6 per cent while the dropout of children after primary level enrollment is 60 per cent. The per capita energy consumption (kg of oil equivalent) is 201 while the newspaper circulation per 1,000 is 19.8 (The World Bank, 1988).

India is a secular country though it has the predominance of Hindus (82.7 per cent). Christians constitute 2.4 per cent of the total population while Sikhs constitute 2.0 per cent. Buddhists are only 0.7 per cent while Jains form a 0.5 per cent of the total population, the other groups are 0.4 per cent of the total population. Hindus alone have about 2378 main castes, sub-castes or *Jatis*. There are about 3,734 Backward Castes in India out of which the number of the Scheduled Castes is 1086 while that of Scheduled Tribes is 566 (India's Backward Classes Commission) Linguistic diversity is reflected in having as many as 1,652 spoken languages (1961) later on classified as 16 scheduled (one English and 15 Indian languages) and 91 other languages (India, Registrar General, 1987). People of India Report, (Anthropological Survey of India), has stated as many as 4635 communities (400 tribal groups and 1108 scheduled caste groups constituting 8 per cent and 16.4 per cent respectively of the total population) and more than 400 linguistic groups.

All this diversed population in age, sex, literacy, caste or class background and religious adherence are spread out in twenty-five States and seven Union Territories administered through more than 500 districts. People are wedded to parliamentary democracy as a form of governance and have witnessed 51 years of independence and 48 years of republic sovereignty through a Constitution which aimed to secure for its citizens social and economic justice, equality of status and opportunity; assuring the dignity of the individual. These aims were pursued mainly through Five-Year Plans. Presently, we are in the Ninth-Five-Year Plan with a couple of plan holidays and an annual rolling plan in between. By and large, the transfer of power after elections in the Indian State remained peaceful, however the electoral politics dominated over the developmental politics and the game of numbers played havoc with the developmental plans despite a rise in GNP or per capita income. The majority of the people, especially in the rural areas got marginalized mainly due to low income and regional disparities, malnourishment, increasing poverty, low literacy and health facilities. Population rise further retarded the developmental process. A brief review of some of the basic demographic, economic, socio-cultural and political data highlights that India through her developmental efforts over the last five decades, has pulled herself out of the preindependent stagnation stage of economy, yet the increasing population, increasing dependency ratio, poor health and nutritional status, diversity of population (religion, language and regionwise), low level of literacy and newspaper circulation, low work force participation, low female literacy and female participation rate, affect the socio-economic development of this vast nation very badly. This is further accentuated by the skewed distribution of the agricultural land (the overall average size of land holding is about 2.3 hectares, while the majority, 70 per cent of holdings, are of less than 2 hectares), uneven monsoon as the most part of country (72 per cent) receives rain less than 127 cms a year and is besides further likely to be affected by drought conditions, (of the total area under cultivation—173.3 million hectares, only 25 per cent is under irrigation) dismal picture of land reforms, lack of infrastructural facilities, increasing malnourishment and poverty, lack of adequate institutional structure, unemployment among youth, employment and underemployment of the educated youth, health and education problems especially of the rural population, and large family size. These issues and many more now in operation at the global level due to globalization of market economic forces such as end of cold war, reduction in arm race, GATT (General Agreement on Tariffs and Trade) and

World Trade Organization, multipolar regions of economic power, peace dividends, liberalism and competition, ethnic resurgence and political turmoil and instability, may pose a challenge to the planners and administrators of the country for a sustainable development programme or policy.

Indian Society: A Panorama of Continuity and Change

The modal value pattern of an Indian society is that of Hindus while other religious and cultural groups also contribute towards its richness, and diversified variations observed in it. Despite many onslaughts from the Aryans through Mughals to British colonists, Hinduism has survived. The inner consistency of certain values of Hinduism is considered responsible for its survival and perpetuation.

Secondly, Indian life is village life as nearly 74 per cent of population is settled in about six lakh villages, having distinct features, differentiating them from the urban settlements. The history of a village in India is as old as the history of this nation. A village settlement had to be opted by a large section of people as a consequence of settled agriculture, domestication of animals, and family-kinship complex efforts towards production and consumption of goods and services for a self-sufficient living. Besides rural is differentiated from urban in terms of its geo-physical location, spatial distributions of households based on kinship-family ties and close interaction between individuals and families. The occupational structure rests on agriculture, the informal clientele system is formalized through established traditions, conventions and institutions; control and authority is based on ascription and the belief system on faith and conviction of religious ethics and themes (Mehta, 1984).

Thirdly, the Indian philosophy revolves around the total truth about reality as a whole and towards the integration, interpretation and unification of knowledge regarding experiences such as religious, ascetic, social, moral and scientific. The immaterial is given precedence over material. Material life is considered only as a means to accomplish the ultimate reality. The Hindu view of life, further refuses to be exclusive and is willing to accept other evidence and experiences as a basis of truth. This openness has made Indian thought as flexible and tolerant.

Besides, the Holy book Gita, highlights the concept of 'self' as absolute acting without attachment or rewards, tolerance, feeling alike in pleasure or pain, performance of one's duties, transmigration of soul and reincarnation of the self and surrender or humble submission to 'Brahman'. These thoughts and values have been transmitted from one generation to the next in the Indian society and have largely shaped the socio-cultural, economic and political life of the people (Bishop, 1975).

In the above backdrop, one may like to examine certain continuities and change in the Indian society especially related to institutions such as religion, caste and class stratifications, family, marriage, economy and polity and cultural ethics and values.

Religion is a core element in one's social life. Faith in deities or any Holy Book, has guided the way of life for centuries but over the years, it is observed that religion has ramified through various phases and is ultimately turning outside in. This tendency on the part of people of different religious beliefs and adherences, is becoming fundamental in structure and form. So far, the minority religious groups in this country (Muslims, Sikhs, Christians) were having a feeling of insecurity. At the most, they were trying to be protectionists but even the majority community consciousness about Hindutva led to Mandir-Masjid disputes at Ayodhya. The military action in the Sikh Golden Temple at Amritsar and Chirag-e-Sharif Masjid in Kashmir are other instances which speak of the politicization of religion in the Indian society. Some political parties are speaking about politics without religion but history suggest evidences contrary to that.

Because of politicization of religion, people tend to become more religious than before and this is evident by their number in temples, mosques, churches and gurdwaras as well as by their exclusive participation in the respective festivities of their religious group. Philosophical contents of the religions are becoming less important whereas rituals and mythological components are being over dramatized. Will the protagonists of religions of various faiths and shades, instead of fighting among themselves, for their selfish ends, outreach themselves to the poor and suffering people? Religion should serve the human beings rather than becoming master of them.

Another significant institutional structure in our society is the pattern of stratification based generally on age, sex, physical strength, caste or class dimensions. In Indian society, age is still a factor to reckon with. Elderly people are respected and consulted in family matters. Maturity, experience and considerate thinking are still upheld. However, in urban centres, especially in metropolitan cities and to a limited extent in rural areas, youth has acquired a self-identity and persons younger in age tend to assert, take lead in decision making, are innovative, dynamic and exhibit a generation gap with the elders. They generally deviate from certain norms, and express behavioural patterns which are Western, European and non-Indian. Indian society being patriarchal, has all along been a male dominated society. The status of woman in certain respects has been that of an oppressed, discriminated and exploited person. Although in Vedic times, a woman was considered a puritan, a Sati Savitri or Sita, embodiment of virtue, dedication and 'sacrifice' yet over the historical epochs, her status has been almost equated to that of an outcaste. She is supposed to keep herself indoors without questioning the authority of man. She cannot express her opinion, take part in family decisions or decisions related to her work setting and is expected to perform her household chores without grudge. Education and employment were immaterialised dream for her. These elements still do persist in rural as well as in urban India. However, women movements, education and employment opportunities, western feminist ideas, social reforms related to widow remarriage, condemnation of "Sati Pratha", constitutional equality, industrializing and urbanizing influences and modern values, have emancipated many women from the domination of men and they have been able to achieve some equality. But women are not a homogeneous group. They are represented by rural, urban, educated, uneducated, working and non-working women and each of these groups has to grapple with issues, problems and contradictions that are different from the other groups. This makes their emancipation a difficult proposition. Among the urban educated working class, the divorce rate is high and marital discord is on the rise. Among metropolitan cities, the institution of marriage has taken a secondary place. Living together is observed quite common among the youth. In spite of changing status of women, female infanticide, sex determination tests, female malnourishment and other similar factors are affecting sex ratio in our country. As such, there is a need to change the attitudes of men towards women. Without this change, a woman's status in a patriarchal society will not improve. Most of the woman work because of economic compulsions while others do so to get feminist elitist status. Both the roles of man and woman will have to be complementary and supplementary rather than contradictory and without such compliance of roles, the status of woman will remain as of now.

Physical strength remained a thing of the past as a factor stratifying Indian society. A person's valour and skill in hunting, archery, wrestling or in any other adventurous activity was considered a matter of pride for him. But with the advancement of the society, these things were pushed to the background. However, with the politicization of Indian society and with electoral politics assuming significance in Indian political life, musclemen are coming into the forefront of Indian social life. Over the years, one gets the impression that we have returned to the law of the "Jungle" where the will of the "lathi" rather than of vote prevails. The game of numbers has given rise to such a situation in Indian politics and there is an urgent need of electoral reforms.

Caste and class are two other significant dimensions of social stratification in Indian society. Research evidence suggests that in the Indian context caste and class inheres in each other. With codification of castes by Manu, social life in our society got differentiated. The social relationships between different castes acquired a clientele pattern known as "Jajmani" system. The services to various castes were hierarchically arranged in the society on the basis of nature of their activities and on the concept of purity-pollution dichotomy. Hierarchical ranking of castes brought about the concept of social status or prestige based on the relative positions of the caste groups. Subsequently, the dominance or influence of these castes was not determined as much by purity-pollution dimension but the possession of land and amount of land possessed by various caste groups, became significant indicators of dominance especially in the village setting. As such, all those caste groups who could acquire land or inherit land, became powerful and the landless and artisan castes entered into a "Jajmani" relationship with these powerful groups and remained in the subservient position.

On the above basis, we can say that caste and class dimensions got correlated. In the urban setting, education became a critical factor for entering into diversified occupational groups enjoying differentiated ranking, prestige or status depending upon the income, authority or influence dimension. Caste is characterized by hierarchy, ranking, endogamy, and commensal relationships. Over the last five decades, there are many variations in the caste system due to education, occupational mobility, migration and constitutional provisions for the welfare of various groups. Due to reservation policy for persons belonging to lower castes, scheduled tribes and backward castes in education, employment and election, many people have climbed higher ladders of caste hierarchy. Despite many ramifications in the caste structure, there are two distinct features which have emerged, over the years. One pertains to increasing role of caste in electoral politics, when V.P. Singh became the champion of backward castes and classes and was all out to implement the recommendation of the Mandal Commission. The offensive was against the 'power and wealth' domination of minority upper castes. The stock argument was that when the left parties could play class as a factor in politics, why cannot caste be made instrumental for the same purpose? This has dangerous implications as caste identities have given rise to other parochial primordial ties such as religion, language, territory and communal affiliations that may help disintegrate rather than integrate the Indian society.

However, the second distinct feature is the endogamous nature of caste which persists despite the onslaught of modernization. There may be same exceptions, that too in the metropolitan centres of the country where caste considerations may be secondary in contracting marriages, but by and large, the marriages in Indian society are guided by caste considerations. This is observed even among educated urbanites who are diffident to move out of the caste confines in respect of marriage. However, at the commensal level, people do share each other's caste groups but at the normative level, behaviours are restricted.

Over the years, due to developmental activities, agricultural advancement, industrialization, education, social mobility, occupational diversification, expansion of trade and commerce, constitutional provisions and electoral democracy, a mass of middle class has emerged in the Indian society.

P.V. Narasimha Rao, the former Prime Minister of India, made a statement in Tokyo on 23rd June, 1992 that Japanese businessmen have a strong 200 million middle class Indians as a base for their market at a time when traditional European and North American markets are tending to be retreating into protectionism (Thakur, 1993). In economic terms, three different strata have emerged in India. We have, in the first instance, a reasonably affluent middle class and upper middle class, constituting nearly 25 per cent of the population or about 200 million. The second tier is that of 40 per cent or 330 million who have received some benefits of growth, both economically and politically since independence but manages a level of living which is uncomfortable but yet not disparate. The third stratum is that of bottom 35 per cent or 258 million, who live still in poverty (Panandikar and Umashankar, 1994).

Despite emergence of class dimensions in the Indian society, there is no clear cut polarization of class structures. Even in States where left parties have been in governance or in power (Left Front in West Bengal), class ideology gets falsified as most of the leaders of their high rank and file are influenced by the caste ideology, secondly most of them come from the upper caste groups. This contradiction apart, one general observation is that as a consequence of development initiatives and modernization process, certain groups and certain individuals within these groups who were 'go-getter' type, availed the developmental benefits both in agricultural and industrial sectors of the economy. But to what extent, caste has changed into class in the Indian setting is a big question mark. Caste and kinship solidarities are emerging and there is resurgence of ethnicity factor all over the country. Still, a large majority of the groups are feeling marginalized due to high technological market oriented growth strategies with which they find it difficult to be compatible. As such, there is a tendency on their part to retrench themselves into their respective groups.

Family and marriage are two other significant aspects of Indian social life. Despite a shift from joint family pattern to nuclear family type, one may not find nuclear family in pure form even in urban centres of India. Family ties are extended through first and second generation siblings and there are extensions of relationships between parents and children in and across generations. On important social functions and occasions, there are efforts on the part of all family members, and kinship members to meet. Even on festival like Diwali, efforts are to celebrate these at the core family level. However, economic independence and independent political decisions or decisions pertaining to one's primary nuclear family are the outcome of nuclearization of families. Greater gender equality in family, female education and employment and liberal attitudes in-between sexes have affected the family life. The hold of a patriarch in the family is declining and especially among the educated urban class, group rather than individual decisions are favoured.

In marriage, although monogamy has come to stay as a major form of marriage, yet other forms of contracting or solemnizing marriages are still in practice among certain groups in different parts of the country. There is more of moral laxity observed among families in upper and lower strata of the society while the middle stratum remains to be the norm setter for the society. Personal rather than parental's choice is on the rise to in selection of partners. Economic compulsion for some has motivated them to have employed partners. Small families rather than large are preferred. Divorce rate and marital discords are on the increase. Incompatibility between partners due to different value orientation, gender assertion and dowry demands are increasing day by day. These phenomena are more pronounced in urban rather than in rural setting.

Economy and polity for the functioning of any society go hand in hand. India had for a decade, a stagnant agricultural and industrial era. People were mostly at the subsistence level of economy and the growth rate was sluggish, slow and it was labelled as "Hindu" economy. However, after independence,

India started with a command economy which pursued restricted private investments whereas most of the investments in industry, were in the public sector to provide infrastructural needs of development as well as to meet the growing needs of vast population, which hitherto had a low purchasing power. However, agricultural sector was largely in private hands. The command economy had an industrial policy which was pursued largely through licensing and permit systems. It involved inspectional rights of the bureaucratic organizations and the control on industry resulted in poor industrial growth rate in the private sector.

Even the public sector organizations became inefficient due to heavy inputs and low turnover. Thus corruption and inefficiency became the twofold detrimental factors for industrial growth. Income and regional disparities, illiteracy, malnourishment and poverty dimensions of a large population, despite a rise in GDP, become apparent. Agriculture sector also added to these problems. Though we had record food production over the years, due to consistent fall of monsoons on the Indian soil, yet the distribution system remained inadequate.

Further, due to the skewed distribution of land holdings and a large number of cultivators being small and marginal farmers, the income levels of the poor could not rise above the level of decent living. The government headed by P.V. Narasimha Rao within a few months of coming into office announced a new industrial policy. This radical liberalization policy was with a view to take stock of the economic crisis of balance of payments in 1991 and to reduce state interventions in the industrial growth and expansion of trade. So there is a move away from the command economy and a move towards the market economy to encourage international competitiveness and promote foreign investments. These reforms have not been as speedy as the situation of Indian economy warranted but the political compulsions seem to be suggesting a cautious approach. Globalization and liberal market economic approaches have been criticized by the left parties CPI(M) and CPI as well as by the rightist parties like BJP who speak of 'Swadeshi' as the cardinal basis for India's economic development. Interestingly enough, the left government in West Bengal is now wooing foreign investors to establish industries so as to capture capital for their State development.

Notwithstanding the radical, liberal changes in the India's economic development, the question arises whether these efforts will lift people above the poverty line or not. Can the market economy be a panacea for all kinds of ills of Indian society, namely, poverty, illiteracy, malnourishment and unhealthy living conditions of people? Instead of being only a welfare State, which most of the market economies are, we shall have to evolve a strategy of development which should take into account the local conditions, issues and problems and through people's participation in economic activities suitable to them get over some of the developmental problems of the large majority of poor in this country. But, there are political compulsions, as after the end of cold war and downfall of Soviet Union and other Eastern Socialist countries in the 1990s, nearly one quarter of India's export was depended upon these countries. India shall have to reorient their foreign policy towards Europe, Japan and USA. This is possible only if India liberalizes her economy at home and open-up to international trade elsewhere (Thakur, 1993).

Indian National Congress, the largest party in India, championed for getting freedom to this country from the colonial rule of the British. Except for two intervals when the break-away Congress groups, the so called Janata Party; gathered momentum with the support of Left Front and BJP, since independence the congress party in its various from and nomenclature has governed the country. At present, BJP with the help of some regional party and some small national party is enjoying power at the centre. But the same lost vote of confidence in the Parliament and fresh elections are now to be held shortly. Indian society, by and large, represent a feudal culture and the interaction of this traditional social structure with the modern realms of democratic forces, has given mixed results and thrown up many contradictions.

In the Indian political set-up, democratic system is imperfect. Here you have poverty coexisting with wealth and equality which is the central element of democracy is a far cry. It is a democracy where education and health are not the functions of income. This democracy is dominated by electoral politics which has brought casteism, communalism, factionalism, linguisticism and regionalism to the forefront. As a consequence of people becoming vote banks, some political parties have gained over the others and non-secular and non-democratic issues like that of Mandir-Masjid, created riotous situation. Terrorism, bomb blasts, State sponsered counter terrorism, Bofors gun deal, security scams, sugar scandal, religious and ethnic strifes, large scale constitutional amendments, reservation and anti-reservation movements, vote rigging and many more events have created crisis of governance for the nation-state. These scandalous pronouncements may be because of lack of education on the part of majority. This factor impacts the smooth functioning of democracy but these are largely due to self-oriented behaviour of individuals at the helm of affairs who for their selfish motives, manipulate, mismanage, institutionalize corrupt and criminalize India's democratic fabric. Electoral reforms, strict vigilance by the Election Commission, greater consciousness among people of human rights, gender equality, common code of language, monitoring of economic activities and strict accountability of people at all levels of responsibility within the well-informed legal framework may reduce some of the crisis situations and move our people towards a civil society. Collective goals and collective responsibility should be pursued at the cost of individual goals to avoid chaotic conditions that may arise, if things are made to continue the way they are allowed to run the course.

In the last, let it be known that Indian society is torn apart because of changes in her value system. Some of the major values upheld in our society are conciliation or reconciliation, tolerance, sympathy, hierarchy, affection and warmth expressed through sentiments and emotions, belief in Almighty God as a creator, preserver and destroyer of the universe, fructification of actions according to one's deeds (*Karma*), spirituality and belief in reincarnation, mutual help and cooperation, hospitality and concern for the needy and suffering people. However modernization of our society has brought in certain values which are disturbing the Indian social order. These are self-orientation, individuality, intolerance, hostility, conflict, rudeness, rationality, scienticism, materialism and achievement-orientation.

Some of these values may be conducive for individual growth and development of the society. But these values need not be adopted at the cost of our traditional values. In fact, the traditional values, instead of being rejected should be evaluated along with modern values and only those values which act as a balance wheel, to our societal system, among the traditional values, should be adopted. Certain values adopted by emancipating educated urban women and young men bring distortion within our culture. The anonymity of the urban culture might have made them permissible but these have negative socializing effects on the young children and to the families of orientation. As a consequence, we have sex abuse, child abuse, juvenile delinquency, violence, theft, burglary, rape, murder, and crimes of varied nature increasing in our society. These, if not controlled either through formal or informal methods may lead to chaotic conditions in the society.

Pang of Poverty and Population Growth: Developmental Crisis

Poverty and population growth, in our context are interrelated. If the incidence of poverty is higher, that may promote a large size of family at the household level to produce more hands and provide a minimum level of living to a poor family. On the other hand, a large size of family needs more food consumption and in the absence of sufficient and necessary production resources, the members of the family may be tilted towards poor living conditions. So there is a vicious circle through which poverty and population growth operates. The macro level situation is also similar. Low income, unemployment, malnourishment, illiteracy, poor health, insanitary living conditions, shanty dwellings, physical and social incapacities are some of the important dimensions of poverty. Landlessness and small land holdings in rural areas are added dimensions.

The incidence of poverty in India was large at the time of independence (60 per cent) while in 1861 it was reported to be 81 per cent (Punit, 1982). Growth may be a necessary condition to reduce poverty but it is an unsufficient condition in all situations. Various estimates placed nearly 50 per cent of India's below the poverty line. Due to developmental efforts of the government through poverty alleviation programmes employment and housing opportunities, at the end of the Seventh Plan, the claim made is that the poverty line has been brought down to 37 per cent. The World Bank has placed 40 per cent of India's population below the poverty line. (The World Bank, 1989). As of 1989, about 29 per cent of the population lived below the poverty line, defined in terms of 2,250 calories per day. (India, Ministry of Health and Family Welfare, 1992). Another interesting statistics provided by the World Bank (World Development Report, 1989) is that the richest 20 per cent of all household population account for 50 per cent of India's expenditure while the 20 per cent poorest account for just 7 per cent of such an expenditure. We have skewed distribution of resources as is reflected by the consumption pattern. There is a vast mass of poor people (about 300 million) and we need to evolve a developmental policy to improve the lot of these people. Close to the heels of poverty, employment is the basic input for poverty alleviation. It is estimated that there would be a rise of 110 million persons in the young adult cohort group of ages 15-29 between 1980 to 2000 as compared to 69 million between 1960 and 1980. This increased young adult population will diverge significantly across regions of the country, with the most rapid growth in the Eastern and Central States. Beyond 2000, this increase will depend upon the declining or rising fertility levels in different regions. These young persons need to be given employment.

Agriculture is the major source of income in India, especially for the poor population. NSS (National Sample Survey, 1983) data indicated that agriculture employed about 64 per cent of total labour force estimated to be 269 million (199 million men + 70 million women) and over three-fourths of the rural labour force, estimated to be 210 million (150 million men + 60 million women). On the other hand, industry (including mining and construction) employed 15 per cent of the labour force while in services hold the remaining 21 per cent (The World Bank, 1989).

During the last two decades, employment has grown at a rate of about 2.2 per cent per annum, but due to a faster increase in labour force (2.5 per cent) the backlog of unemployment has been increasing. Despite, of having an annual growth rate of 5.5 per cent during the last decade as compared to 3.5 per cent in the previous three decades, there is a declining trend in the employment elasticity with respect to GDP growth in the recent years. In the light of above, an accelerated expansion of employment opportunities is necessary for poverty alleviation as well as for effective utilization of human resources for development of the country (Planning Commission, 1992).

The Eighth Five-Year Plan envisages a generation of additional ten million employment opportunities per year on an average or about 3 per cent average annual growth of employment. However the incidence of unemployed in the country may vary from 30 million to 70 million, although the official figure is about 23 million. A relatively high economic growth rate combined with sectoral growth, may provide a higher aggregate employment opportunity. Cropwise and areawise diversified agriculture, wasteland development for cultivation and forestry, rural non-farm sector especially small manufacturing units, rural infrastructure, housing and services are the basic elements of an employment oriented growth strategy. Raising the productivity and income levels of the people in traditional and in the unorganized sectors of economy through self-employment technologies, and access of poor to credit and market institutions, may further improve the prospects of the poor (Planning Commission, 1992).

In addition to above inputs, building physical and social capacities of the poor through fair distribution of essential food to meet nutritional deficiency, health care, sanitary living conditions (supply of safe drinking water and proper disposal of excreta and refuge) ventilated dwellings and acquiring knowledge and skills through formal and non-formal educational methods and media are essential steps that may lift the poor from the state of deprivation, dependence and degradation, in which physically and socio-culturally they have been placed.

Above all, the most important aspect of eradicating poverty from the map of this country is to check population growth. A consistent population growth rate of 2.1 per cent per annum is adding to an additional population of 18 million every year.

Today the population of India is about one billion. The rate of growth has been marginally lower during eighties than what it was during seventies but if this trend is not halted, we shall fail miserably to render social and economic justice to millions of our people.

Despite, India being an early adopter of family planning policy to reduce birth rate, we are confronted with the problem of population explosion. Ever since the First Five-Year Plan in 1951, the budgetary provisions as well outreached to people have been widened in all the subsequent Five-Year Plans. But when the 1971 Census sent an alarming signal of India's population growth rate of 2.25 per cent per annum, then Union Health Minister Dr. Karan Singh, suggested to then Prime Minister Indira Gandhi in October 1975 that in view of rapid population growth, there is a need to introduce some elements of compulsion in the family planning programme in the larger interest of the nation. Later on he came out with a National Population Policy in 1976 which however, could not be implemented; that policy in April 1976 had suggested some bold and drastic measures to contain population growth.

Sanjay Gandhi, the uncrowned king of India, and later Indira Gandhi through her 20-point programme of development (one, of course related to fertility reduction) became champions for checking the population rise. Coercive measures were employed to increase the sterilization of couples (the number of sterilization are reported to rise from 1.3 million in 1974-75 to 2.6 million in 1975-76 and to 8.1 million in 1976-77) while other methods of fertility control such as IUD and condoms showed no increase. However, subsequently after an initial fall, the birth rate showed an upward trend of 33.3 per thousand and remained so till 1985. It is reported that even 1981 Census showed a population growth rate of 2.2 per cent per annum. It was felt by many that India in her history had the highest growth rate during the period 1971-81 (the period in which there was emergency declared in this country and continued for about nineteen months). Later, when the Janta Party came into power in 1977, they declared that new population policy would be based on voluntarism. This led to a decline in the sterilization cases as well as it affected the other schemes of Family Planning

Programme. After Indira's return to power in 1980, the Government came out with a Health Policy in 1983 and promised a new population policy but the latter could not be formulated. Based on the bitter experiences of emergency, the Government pursued a cautious approach. Narasimha Rao's Government again made an effort to come out with a National Population Policy (Panandikar and Umashankar, 1994).

Apart from the electoral politics, another significant factor that affects the fertility control in India is socio-cultural diversity. Because of her population having different religions, castes communities, ethnic identities, linguistic groups, since 1992 (we have 18 officially recognised languages and English language being spoken widely in the country, besides many dialects), varied customs, cultural ethos, idioms and themes and belonging to different economic strata; it is extremely difficult to build up communication strategies and motivate people to limit their family size. A country which is poverty stricken and where the literacy level especially among the females is at the lowest level, there is a need to evolve motivational strategies using media mix to generate new economic tastes and preferences among the people. This is a tremendous task to which the policy planners need to address themselves seriously and with sincerity. Besides we have to tackle some of the socio-cultural determinants of fertility. These are female literacy, age at marriage especially for girls, employment opportunities for women and their status in society. In addition, we need to reduce infant mortality rate, improve health and nutrition of pre-school children and provide comprehensive reproductive health care to the mothers. This would warrant intersectoral coordination and for that to become effective, there is a need for a strong political commitment at all levels. A National Population Policy need to be evolved and it must generate enough boost to make population control a people's initiative.

Adding 18 million mouths to feed every year, out of which nearly one-third belongs to the poverty line, puts a great burden on the developmental front. A higher growth rate would bring forth longer investments which are possible only through larger savings. As such, growth will depend upon the mobilization of resources. We have poor public sector savings in the recent years and the household savings to be transferred to public sector savings is increasingly becoming costly. Thus planning for higher level of investment in view of resource crunch is hitting hard at the developmental plans. Foreign borrowings and aids are not without strings. One who pays the piper calls for the tune. In view of this, we need to have proper fiscal management to raise revenues and restrict expenditures at the Central as well as at the State levels. Subsidies on certain items will have to be done away and there is a need to cut on the defence expenditure as well. In order to contain population to a desirable limit and eradicate or at least reduce the incidence of poverty, there is a need to have a large financial outlay at least in one sector of development, that is education. Education is a critical variable to reduce the acute pangs of poverty and population. Oeschli and Kirk while showing indicators to describe the typical profile of a country at the different stages of demographic transition (using data from Latin America and the Caribbean) suggest that a marked decline in fertility among other things, is associated with (a) literacy rate of 78 per cent, (b) an expectation of life at birth of 60 years, (c) a primary school enrollment ratio of 65 per cent, (d) a labour force in non-agriculture of 52 per cent, (e) an urbanization rate of 40 per cent and (f) a secondary school enrollment of 22 per cent. (Oeschli and Kirk, 1975).

We, in India, have yet to catch up with these indicators. However, Kerala shows remarkable achievements in reducing birth rate and death rate. Female literacy and employment, better sex ratio (it is 1055), health care, and land reforms ensuring greater labour participation rates are some of the factors that have gone into such a success story. It is reported that with 65.7 per cent of its female population literate (1988 data) and 100 per cent of enrollment of girls in the middle schools, Kerala had an estimated crude birth rate of 19.9, a crude death rate of 6.3 and an infant mortality rate of 28 per 1000 live births (Ministry of Health and Family Welfare, 1989). Even the land reforms during the Communist governments and the remittances sent back home by migrants to foreign countries because of better education and skills, have helped in reducing the incidence of poverty in rural areas of Kerala.

Can the developmental crises caused by population growth

and a high incidence of poverty be averted by increasing inputs in education in the plan outlays? To contain children population in schools and to avoid any dropouts, food subsidy as an incentive at the school level may be given as a trial. Subsidies of various other nature and public distribution systems, are already bred with inefficiency, corruption and nepotism. Education also provides knowledge and skills to persons and they develop their social capacities for greater productivity. Research evidence in different countries suggest that farmers with primary level education have proved more productive than the farmers who are uneducated. Health care and better nutrition status will further enhance the social capacity of the poor. As such, economic measures alone will not suffice for development purposes and we shall have to bank upon human resource development through correct management of vast mass of human beings who have arrived in this country for making a decent living and not just for their mere existence. That would warrant strengthening social services like education and health. Population should be treated as an asset rather than a liability.

Is Sustainable Development a Possibility?

Sustainable development for whom and how long and where? What would be the scenario beyond sustainable development? These questions need serious debate to arrive at some consensus for sustainable development of the developing nations. Sustainable development has a time dimension. At least, it should continue till the next generation of people assume the responsibility. Further, sustainable development could be at global, national or local level. Sustainable development came into limelight mainly because the other paradigms of development such as capitalist growth model and socialist political economy model, failed to provide a good society to the developing nations. There should be good society without strains or disruptions. These paradigms too had their ideals of a good society. According to first paradigm, a good society is one in which people have the most possible goods and services with the least cost, the least effort and the least use of resources. While according to the other paradigm, a good society is one that enables people to meet their basic needs and carry out their preferred social activities (Weaver, 1975). Both these paradigms have been criticized as these provide privileged role to the national elites and brought in strains and disruption in the developing as well as in the developed societies. Another group of theorists are pinning their hope on the ethnodevelopment strategy based on grassroot socio-political movements and popular culture. Further, a group of scholars are seized with a model of communication policy that shall promote politico-economic and socio-cultural negotiation and integration to form a common national culture for development (Mehta, 1992).

As a consequence of industrializations and urbanization, there has been a large scale destruction as well as overutilization of natural resources. This has resulted in environmental degradation, air and water pollution, acid rain, greenhouse effects due to emission of gases and ozone depletion. These unintended or intended effects of high technology fueled development strategies have been felt more by the people of the developed than that of the developing world. The fallout of this is, that there is a demand for sustainability of planet's resources for the development of the present as well as for the future generation. The developing nations are also being asked by the developed to conserve their natural resources for generation of energy necessary for technological advancement, when their own energy consumption is almost 200 times more than that of developing countries.

It is suggested that some countries of South having tropical and subtropical climate are already at a disadvantage to the countries of the North in the temperate zone as tropical conditions affect the output of human energy, economic development and even the political culture of the developing nations (Bandyopadhya, 1982). Besides, there are limited natural and economic resources, a high population growth while the incidence of poverty in the developing nations is on the rise. In the light of above circumstances, sustainable development for developing nations like India is a difficult proposition. Can that difficulty be converted into a possibility? Sustainable development activities may be time bound but the sustainable development processes should be continuous as they involve future generations. In view of India opening up to market economic forces and globalization syndrome, the whole planning exercise shall have to be revamped and only economically viable schemes in consistent with people's needs and participation should be promoted for generating additional resources within the community. Instead of Five-Year Plan, an annual plan may be desirable. Private investments may be getting a boost but investments in infrastructural development have to be monitored through efficient management of public sector undertakings.

India may have limited coal and oil resources but we have plenty of sun and air. Renewable energy systems shall have to be given priority and these resources shall have to be exploited to the maximum extent. Means of communication especially road network, larger irrigation outlays, dry land farming, soil conservation, agricultural development especially in eastern regions, electrification of railways, improvement in waterways, check on water and air pollution, treatment of industrial-effluents for refuse, proper sewerage and garbage disposal and that of industrial waste, land reforms, diversification of agriculture and changes in cropping patterns, may go a long way in making India's development sustainable. Further in India's context, flood, drought and deforestation shall have to be managed. However, all these activities would entail technology transfer as well as building up technologically, sound manpower indigenously for sustaining these activities. This would involve communication and negotiated understandings with the developed world through coalition groups such as, NAM, SAARC and Group of 77, etc., of the developing nations. Technological development apart, there is a need for integrating various social concerns related to literacy, child survival, nutritional status of pre-school children and women development. Reduction in birth rate and minimum health care are crucial elements in sustainable development to improve the quality and productivity of the population. Integration of indigenous medicines and homeopathy with western medicine and encouraging health cooperatives in our villages maybe hard options for us to improve the health delivery system (Mehta, 1992).

The parameters of sustainable development outlined above may be necessary but they are insufficient as such. These need to be planned and implemented in a coordinated manner so that we can be technologically innovative for conserving our natural resources, simultaneously for our welfare and for the welfare of our future generation. This is easier said than done. It would call forth strong commitment on the part of politicians, bureaucrats, intellectuals and non-governmental organizations at various levels. Inefficiency, corruption, nepotism, favouritism, psychophancy, self-oriented behaviour, gender inequality, inhuman considerations, jealousy and violation of human rights are becoming the order of the day. These need to be changed to more humane consideration, concern for others, altruism and welfare of needy and sufferings. Can we look towards Buddha and Gandhi, the emissaries of love and humanness? They might have become irrelevant in the modern world but they are the real torch bearers for unification of Man with Man and for the unification of Man with the cosmos. This philosophical ending may not sound Utopian but only ideas can be translated into action by the ingenious Man, who has progressed towards a civilization, now feels threatened to fall under its own weight.

Collective welfare rather than welfare of an individual should be the sole aim. Let the individual stop vulgarizing himself or herself any more and work towards the welfare of the society. We have a rich tradition and a cultural heritage and we need to revert to it sincerely. With people's movements, Indian minds and intellects can be made to work towards that end. Deconcentration and decentralization of power to make people's movements a success shall have to be accepted as a way of administration of resources.

In the above backdrop and keeping in view the contemporary changing in Indian society, sustainable development may not be an impossible proposition but a difficult one. Crisis, strifes, conflicts and tensions are part of the development process but we have to manage every thing with an aim to push them towards the larger welfare of the society, on a well-informed basis. The given platitude of sustainable development in the Indian context is not encouraging and that may give us mixed results, some may gain while a large number may get pains. Our efforts should be to reduce pains and enlarge gains for many through bloodless surgical operations and painless therapy. This would warrant delicate handling of the ill society through the skills of an efficient managerial surgeon, be it a politician, bureaucrat, intellectual or a leader of the NGO.

Beyond sustainable development if the operation of the Indian society could be successfully performed, then one could visualize certain elements of a civil society based on a concern for a larger conglomeration, using common code of language, observing legal system supported by the constitutional framework in toto and evolving institutions which cut across the parochial ties such as caste, class, race, language, region and ethnic identities, to promote communitarianism among people. Only then, the sustainable development beyond it, can hope for "Society as a Community". It is an ideal which is difficult to achieve but we can today make efforts to move towards that end for a better India tomorrow. This may be possible if developmental politics take over the electoral politics and we evolve a development paradigm based on our values and keeping in view of our own limited resources rather than largely influenced by Euro-American models. This would require a thorough analysis of Indian society for a synthesis or interrelatedness of factors that may be managed for the development of the society. Let the social scientists take it as a challenge and rise to the occasion instead of politicking in scholarship. An analysis of paradigm shift from socialistic pattern to development based on market economic forces will not suffice. A new paradigm relevant to our emerging scenario is what the social scientists should strive for, through an interdisciplinary approach.

References

Bandyopadhyaya, Jayantanuja, (1982), *North Over South: A Non-western Perspective of International Relations,* New Delhi, South Asian Publishers Pvt. Ltd.

Bishop, Donald, H., (1975), (ed.), Indian Thought: An Introduction, New Delhi, Wiley Eastern Pvt. Limited.

India, Backward Classes Commission, (1980), Report, Delhi, Controller of Publications.

India, International Institute for Population Studies, (1994), Bombay, *National Family Health Survey.*

India, Ministry of Health and Family Welfare, (1989), New Delhi, *Family*

Welfare Programme in India, Yearbook 1987-89.

India, New Delhi, Ministry of Health and Family Welfare, (1992), *Health Information of India,* 1992.

India, Planning Commission, (1992), *Eighth Five-Year Plan Documents.*

India, Registrar General, (1987), New Delhi. *Level, Trends and Differential in Fertility,*

Mehta, S.R., (1984), *Rural Development Policies and Programmes: A Sociological Perspective,* New Delhi, Sage Publication.

Mehta, S.R., (1992), (ed.), *Communication and Development: Issues and Perspectives,* Jaipur, Rawat Publications.

Mehta, S.R., (1992), *Society and Health: A Sociological Perspective,* New Delhi, Vikas Publishing House Private Limited.

Oeschli, F, and Kirk, (1975), "Modernization and the Demographic Transition in Latin America and Caribbean," *Economic Development and Cultural Change,* Vol. 23, No. 3.

Panandiker, V.A. Pai, Umashankar, P.K., (1994), "Fertility Control and Politics in India", in Jason L. Finkle and C. Alison McIntosh (eds), *The New Politics of Population: Conflict and Consensus in Family Planning,* New York, The Population Council.

Punit, A.E., (1982), *Profile of Poverty in India,* Delhi, B.R. Publishing Corporation.

Thakur, Ramesh, (1993), "Restoring India's Economic Health", *Third World Quarterly,* Vol. 14, No. 1.

Weaver, James H., (1975), *Economic Development: Two Paradigms,* Washington D.C., U.S.A.I.D. Transcript of a talk.

World Bank, (1989), *India: Poverty, Employment and Social Services,* Washington D.C., U.S.A.

World Bank, (1989), *World Development Report,* New York, Oxford University Press.

13

Social Aspects of Development

Aspects of Dynamics of Development

Whenever we want to study the dynamics of a phenomenon, be it physical, social or cultural, we have to examine the moving forces, physical or mental in any sphere, to account for energising of matter or mind. In physical sciences, dynamics implies mechanism of treating motion in itself and of the motion of bodies or matter under the influence of forces that activate motion.

In the physical science, we have exact laws postulated to explain motion. For example, in physics we have laws of motion and thermo-dynamics which explain motion in bodies as well as generation of energy. However, the physical system is a closed system. Similarly, in biological sciences, we have laws pertaining to genetic inheritance which determine the shape and form of the body as well as we have Darwinian laws of natural selection of species and their adaptation to the environment.

But what is important is to delineate the interacting forces that may be responsible for the causation of a particular phenomenon. This may be possible in the context of physical and biological systems but in a social system, because of varied complexities and uncertainties, it may be difficult to identify the exact patterns of interaction between social actors whose relationships are contingent upon "significant others", personality correlates, situations and contexts of interaction, and patterns of agencies and institutions in which the interactions take place over time and space as well as on the external environment in which the internal system is located. Since in a generic sense, development means advancement, progress, expansion of resources, better control of environment and growth, we want to examine the development of a social system with all its complexities and uncertainties. We have to analyse the interdependence of all parts of the system which have symmetrical or asymmetrical relationships with one another to integrate certain essential elements through cultural consensus to accomplish the societal goals. The dissensions within the social system are taken care of through control mechanisms evolved within, while the externalities of the external environmental system are absolved through adaptation.

This structural-functional perspective of a society or the corollary of it, the "Modernization" paradigm, does not treat development as static in absolute terms inasmuch as the social system moves, through various differentiation processes, from simple to a complex institutional form. However, the main limitation of this perspective is that structures are given and social actors are expected to perform their roles within these structures. However, the conflict perspective or the dependency theory based on neo-Marxist ideology advocates people's protests and movements through their mobilization for altering relationships in favour of the oppressed and exploited in the Third World nations, to reduce socio-economic inequalities in between the developed and the underdeveloped countries. This kind of mobilization speaks for treating development as a dynamic concept as the social forces have to be energized to move upwards the underdeveloped people through their own motivations and efforts. However, the main dilemma lies in altering the power equation of the elites and the masses. This is easier said than done. Unless, people are empowered to develop themselves through acquiring necessary knowledge and skills, they cannot alter the established and institutionalized relations in between different groups.

Man, as a rational human being, is also considered as a meaning creating being. As such, according to symbolic interactionist perspective, he is capable of choosing the best out of the available alternatives to take an appropriate action that suits his goals, aspirations and requirements. However, there is a risk of the action being guided by personal than societal factors and that may create a problem of social order in the society due to conflicting values of the people.

Notwithstanding the merit or demerit of the sociological

perspective in delineating development as a dynamic concept, apart from an individual's orientation, one has to take into account a societal perspective. Such a perspective has, no doubt, to energise the individual as well as the collective motivation of people, to move the society towards commonly arrived goals of advancement or progress. This can be accomplished either through evolutionary or revolutionary methods. However, the consequences of dynamics of development will be different in the two cases.

Although the post-modernists through their critique of "Modernity" have called for an end to it, yet in the later works of Jurgen Habermas, it is established that "the much criticized Enlightenment legacy, the so-called 'project of modernity', can and must be reconstructed, and requires to be viewed as incomplete, not abandoned" (Scambler, 1996).

The 'Modernization' paradigm failed because it could not provide the rational organization of everyday life for the creation of a good society. For Habermas (1984), Weber's concepts of rationality and rationalization are used in restricted sense and these have been insufficiently abstracted. Further, he submits that different value spheres are increasingly becoming irreconcilable mainly because of "selection rationalization" due to growth and dominance of the capitalist economy and State bureaucracy (Brand, 1990).

Habermas's (1984, 1987) argument is that the universality of rationality depends upon formal or procedural concept of rationality based on linguistic term in the twentieth century philosophy. As such, reason cannot be considered as based on subject-object relations of the philosophy of consciousness but on the subject-subject relations of communication actions. Communication action which means an action oriented to understanding and consensus, is contrasted with strategic action or action oriented to success through manipulation or coercion (Scambler, 1987). This theory of communicative rationality by Habermas provides a critique of Weber's restricted concept of rationalization which occurred in the Occident as inevitable but in fact, was contingent and selective, that is why, he advocates 'selective' rationalization to rationalization as such.

In line with the neo-functionalists, Habermas argues that

societal differentiation has generated four subsystems: the economy, the state, the public sphere and the private sphere. There is basic "uncoupling" between the economy and the state, constituting the system. They are normatively characterized by strategic action while the public and the private spheres, constituting the 'lifeworld' are normatively marked by communicative action. According to Habermas, the four sub-systems are interdependent in the sense that each is specialized in terms of what it produces but depends on others for what it does not produce. The economy, produces 'money', the state 'power', the public sphere 'influence' and the private sphere, 'the commitment.' These products or 'media' are traded between sub-systems, that is, the economy depends on the state to establish legal institutions as private property and contract and on the public lifeworld to influence consumption patterns, and on the private lifeworld to provide a committed labour force, and itself sends money into each of the subsystems. It is suggested that as the 'system' and the 'lifeworld' become clearly marked, the media (products) of the former tend to progressively dominate the latter. This is what Habermas, considers as the 'colonization of the lifeworld' (Crook et al., 1992).

In short, the dynamic of development means that the 'system' rationalization outstrips the rationalization of 'lifeworld', hence the reference to 'selective rationalization'. However, the rationalization of the lifeworld implies an increase in the scope of communicative action, and to the growth of communicative rationality. The logic of development allows for further rationalization of the lifeworld through a reinstitution of its public sphere, the agents of such reinstitution being the 'new' social movements (Scambler, 1996).

In the context of the developing nation, if the development has to be culture specific, then the dynamic of development can be considered within the conceptual framework of "system" and "lifeworld", provided by Habermas. Although in the system, Habermas suggests fundamental linkages between the economy and the state, yet in relation to developing nations these are guided by historical circumstances and traditional social structures and value systems of these nations.

The state apparatuses were managed by oligarchic, autocratic and power centred bureaucratic organizations whose sole interest was the operations of the economy totally in favour of the ruling class. A large mass of people were on subsistence agriculture while the colonists and the expertriates benefitted most from the plantation and extraction industries. The comparative advantages which the developed countries had in trades squeezed the developing countries of their resources and when a change in the demand side was made without a change in the supply, the resultant effect was underdevelopment.

However, after the independence of the developing nations from the yoke of colonists, growth strategies on the pattern of western development model were introduced to boost up agricultural production and industrial growth. However, the feudal and the cultural systems of these nations in interaction with modern industrialising and urbanising influences brought in many contradictions which gave more problems of development than solving some of them.

The system, constituting the economy and the state, could make some dent in public sphere by increasing demand for consumerism, yet it failed to increase private sphere due to lack of generation of labour commitment. This resulted in lower productivity in these nations. Despite increase in GNP, these nations failed to tackle the problems of poverty, unemployment, illiteracy and malnourishment among a vast majority of their people.

Development of a nation does not depend only on capital and labour but also on the amount of land and other natural resources, a nation has. That is why, it is suggested that a cultural specific paradigm of development for a nation or a group of nations should be sought rather than conceiving a universal paradigm of development. But more than that, development to a large extent depends upon technology and entrepreneurship. These two basic inputs of development have been observed to be scarce. The "lifeworld", which constitutes the public sphere and private sphere should mobilize people to acquire entrepreneurship and to learn technology appropriate to their needs so that the rising consumer demands are met adequately. Not only that, the 'lifeworld' has to exact demands from the system (the economy and the state) to create cultural conditions for greater private commitment at different levels to match with the public sphere. This would need 'selective rationalization' on the part of agencies and agents who give impetus to new social movements. However, in the dynamic of development, the system, (the economy and the state) should be receptive to these movements and reinstitutionalize or structure new institutions to advance themselves towards a better society.

The main hurdle observed in most of the developing nations is the unstable political and leadership structures. In order to maintain the power positions, the leadership structures have undermined even the economy of these nations inasmuch as the economic institutions, instead of guiding the politicians for creating a good society, are dictated to suit the interests of the power holders. Four recent cross-section studies on economic growth have verified that lack of civil and political liberties is negatively correlated with economic growth. It is reported that for the 115 market economies, studied over a period of 1960-80, the politically open societies advocating civic and economic liberty grew three times the rate of growth than other societies in which this freedom was restricted (Haan and Siermann, 1996).

In the above backdrop, there is an urgent and immediate need to unleash the 'lifeworld' forces in the private and public spheres through mobilization of new movements based on 'selective rationalization' of the agents and agencies so as to transform the economy and the state for restructuring the society towards a better material and moral order. This brings us close to a "participatory" paradigm of development for the developing nations.

Development, instead of imposed from above, should spring up from the heart of the people. This would warrant moving beyond economic growth and going in for social analysis for social development and social change. Social analysis needs to be used to explain the social fabric, design the social goals and chart the path of collective action (Cernea, 1996).

Social analysis also helps in the application of a sociological theory to tackle development problems. It is in this sense that Malinowski suggested that the theory becomes practical when it allows a grip on empirical reality (Malinowski, 1961). If we have to provide a comprehensive social analysis of a developing nation, then not only the theoretical constructs, but also the methods of Sociology and Anthropology must be combined as without adequate analysis of the social structure, no synthesis in the form of a development policy can be provided. This brings us back to the question of the Sociology of Development. What Sociology? What Development?

Academic sociology has been mainly concerned with studies of social consequences of technical progress and economic development particularly the abrupt changes observed in traditional societies and the formation of new social groups including new classes. Besides, some studies deal with the relationships between religious systems and economic changes. Analysis has also been done in the role of local actors (peasants, workers, intellectual or political elites, middle classes, etc.) in the transformation of their societies.

This is what is a 'dynamic sociology' close to the concept of Sociology of Development and the thrust in the franchophonic tradition has been on the continuous relationship between 'dynamics within' and 'dynamics from without', between 'tradition' and modernity; among the various levels of the economic, political and symbolic spheres and between the fragility of equilibria and the trial and error of innovation. Among the French sociologists, the thrust in Sociology of Development has been on the need for technical and economic progress, and thus for corresponding changes in social structures and cultural systems. But, the North American, Sociologists relied heavily on the "Modernization" theories which were particularly evolutionistic, ethnocentric and economistic. It is also suggested that in fact, there are two sociologies of development, one 'Africanist' school focusing on the problems related to restructuring of rural societies, with basic development of the construction of new states and the 'Americanist' school, concerned with social classes, social movements and political systems (Haubert, 1991).

This clearly highlights the need for treating development of a nation in reference to its cultural conditions. But in the context of globalization process unleashed by the technological superiority, market economic forces and the freedom syndrome of the western developed nations, the dynamics of development 'within' a developing nation, cannot be sealed off from dynamics 'outside' these nations. This is a dilemma which needs to be tackled by the coalition of the developing nations, making demands on the developed nations for equity, social justice and probity.

Without a negotiated understanding between the developed and developing nations along a horizontal plane, the development of the developing nations, even if they manage their internal dynamics of the economy, the state, the public and the private sphere, will remain a difficult proposition. Nuclear power, nuclear warheads and weaponization are likely to disturb military power balance in between nations and regions and may be counter-productive to the peace dividends obtained during the last half a century or so. This may halt or impede the progress and advancement of the developing nations.

The Indian Social Reality

Construction of a social reality in an objective manner is a difficult task. The researcher, while attempting to do is always handicapped by his personal assumptions, structural and cultural perceptions and upholding of certain values dear to him or her. The only way one could validate or invalidate one's construction of social reality is to compare the results of observations made by others. During the last half of century or so, many social scientists/researchers, both foreign and indigenous, have made several attempts to construct the social reality of the Indian society.

Foreign scholars, by their advantage of studying the "other cultures", were in an advantageous position to objectively point out the contrasting situations to their own cultures. But they seemed to miss some of the significant dimensions of our social life which provided core elements to our societal structure. However, the indigenous sociologists and anthropologists analysing the Indian society, did show ingenuity in highlighting some of the significant aspects of social life, be it religious, family, marriage, economy, polity or tradition-modernity syndrome related to value orientations of people. But they also took some of the aspects of our social life as granted and showed scant concern to some of the other issues.

In the post-independence era, the sociologists and anthropologists in our country got seized with development issues related to agricultural and industrial growth, expansion of trade and commerce, peasant movements, protest and social unrest, entrepreneurship, education, health and issue of population control due to initiatives taken by planned development efforts. Many of the researches undertaken, were reflective of the socio-economic and political consequences of the development efforts for the intended beneficiaries and in a few cases, attempts were also made to examine the causation of some of the significant social phenomena associated with the development initiatives.

These studies, by and large, remained within the realm of building a body of sociology of knowledge to depict the empirical reality. The methods employed by researchers were inductive, deductive and deductive-inductive-deductive based on Euro-American theoretical formulations. These limitations apart, most of these studies did provide insight into the social processes that had gone on or were going on in the contemporary context for displaying the social fabric and contour of our society.

A society is always dynamic and never static. However, a researcher for his analytical purposes has to assume that at the time of his studying a society, the causal factors or the correlating factors to depict social phenomenon remain stationary for that time and cease to move, otherwise analysing a moving or a dynamic society becomes problematic.

Assuming the limitations of sociological theory and methods, an attempt is made here to present before you an approximate construction of Indian social reality. The parameters on which the social reality of our society will be constructed will include geophysical dimensions, population size and density, the economy, the state or the polity, social structural and organizational arrangements, religious adherences and values of the people.

India is a country of continental size in South Asia. Next to China, it is the most populated nation. Being a British colony for nearly two centuries, it has established trade with the near and far off countries in the world. Some of the neighbouring countries such as Myanmar, Nepal, Bangladesh, Pakistan, Sri Lanka, etc. were at one time the part of the Indian subcontinent. Culturally speaking, there are more similarities than differences in between the people of India and people in the neighbouring countries. Physically, she is land locked in the north as well as in the north-east whereas she has a large area covering the western, eastern and southern regions.

Although, India is a peace-loving nation, being a fountain head of an ancient civilization which has discouraged violence and embraced non-violence and peace, In the post-independent era, she has fought one war with China and two wars with Pakistan. Because of our unpreparedness, we humbled ourselves before China but came victorious against Pakistan in both the wars. In the second war against Pakistan, we helped a part of Pakistan, adjacent to our physical setting to carveout Bangladesh. This intensified the latest animosity between India and Pakistan stirred during the partition of two nations in 1947 and they have been raging a proxy war against us through insurgent terrorist activities in different states of our country especially in the Jammu and Kashmir and in the North-East.

Because of perceived threats from India, Pakistan acquired nuclear technology with the help of China who has already got the status of a Nuclear Power State. Both India and Pakistan are yet be recognized as neclear powers by major nuclear power states like U.S.A., Russia, France, Britain and China who are enjoying the permanent membership in U.N. Security Council. Over the years, India too has acquired nuclear technology and the recent blasts indicate that she is heading for a nuclear power status state. Pakistan in its reaction to Indian blasts has gone ahead to outdo the Indian efforts. They carried out six tests proving that they too have nuclear capability. This has invited worldwide criticism against India and Pakistan and some of the developed nations like the U.S.A., Germany, France, Japan, Australia, New Zealand and Canada have announced economic sanctions against both these nations.

The nuclear warheads, weaponization and militarization can lead to a war race in the region and economic sanctions and heavy investment in the destructive weapons paralyse the progress or development of any country especially a developing nation. Besides, border dispute with China, contagious issue of Tibet, water dispute with Bangladesh, anti-Indian feeling in Nepal and ethnic violence in Sri Lanka are some of the geophysical challenges that will keep us on our toes for recurring better relationships with our neighbouring countries. Even within our country, we have a large tract of hill region, desert area, tribal belt and coastal areas which need specific development inputs suitable to their cultural conditions to help people of these regions to overcome their problem of poverty. Development or infrastructural modernization like construction of dams, canals, power, roads, etc., has involuntarily displaced many of the populations of these regions and they need to be rehabilitated in a eco-friendly geo-physical settings of our country.

As a contemporary sociologist, I do not undermine the importance of historical analysis for understanding us in our present set-up, but my contention is to offset the distortions that have crept in the historical analysis. One should be careful in understanding the present objectively so that we could give better direction to our future society. It is in this context that one is compelled to give a priority to the demographic factor in the development of our society. The stark reality is that we are growing at a fast pace and by the end of this century we will cross the 100 crore mark. Is this not alarming? Rapid population growth will complicate social and economic adjustments of people in regard to physical infrastructure, institutions for property right and induced innovations to provide solutions (Mink, 1993). Besides, nearly 40 per cent of the population in this country has been defined to be living in absolute poverty.

This has serious implications from demographic point of view as population size and density of population of poor people in certain states of our country (Bihar, Madhya Pradesh, U.P. and Rajasthan, etc.) because of low literacy level especially among females encouraging early marriage, higher fertility, large family size, age specific mortality' (especially more among females than males), infant mortality, child mortality and migration from the household (especially from rural to urban areas), will affect the development process adversely as a greater number of children would need to be provided with education, nutritious food and health care.

Further, there would be an increase in the number of people seeking jobs. This would need an increase in productive jobs and for that to happen, the investments should grow faster than the labour force. This is unlikely to happen in a country with a large number of unemployed people and underdevelopment. Also limited social mobility, lack of opportunities and lack of access to resources discourage the majority of the poor to participate actively in the development process and they tend to retrench themselves into their religious, linguistic and cultural ethnocentric and ethnic groups. These ethnic formations and identities become susceptible to political mobilization and vote banks for the politicians in a democratic system (Mehta, 1997b).

As such, the population growth, especially among the urban and rural poor, in our setting has not only social, cultural, economic but political consequences as well. It is in this context, a check on population growth has to be given the top priority in a cultural perspective on development through measures acceptable to the people. Education and technological innovations in population control are two critical factors that the state or the polity will have to address to.

However, the main question is whether the economy can meet the needs and rising demands of growing population or not? At the time of independence, India got in legacy a stagnant economy. Agricultural growth was restricted and industrial output was meagre. However, the development efforts during the last five decades both in agriculture and industry despite increasing pressure of population rise, ushered in agricultural growth and industrial development to the level that we could attain self-sufficiency in food grain and be recognized as one of the ten technologically advanced nations of the world. These achievements were stupendous but during the first four decades of development efforts under the command economy, our GNP remained at 3.5 per cent level for long. However, due to economic reform measures through liberalized market economic forces, the economic growth rate showed improvement and attained 7.5 per cent level. But due to coalition politics at the centre, and frequent changes in the Prime Ministerial position, and change of government from one formation of coalition to another, there has been declaration of the overall growth rate to 5 per cent during 1997-98. We have a negative growth rate of agriculture as the production of food grains has slightly fallen (from 199 million to 194 million). Besides, the industrial growth has dipped to 4.2 per cent and our exports are limping downwards during the second successive year, affecting adversely our balance of payments. Inflationary trends are visible again and a fiscal deficit of 6.1 per cent is becoming a cause of concern for the economic development of the country (Gill, 1998).

'Swadeshi' economics of the BJP led government to provide shelter to the Indian entrepreneurship from the onslaught of the multinationals may slow down the private foreign investments. Besides, in the wake of nuclear blasts, the international borrowings may be slashed down due to economic sanctions by some of the developed nations. Moreover, due to disintegration of the erstwhile U.S.S.R., our exports to Russia have been cut down tremendously and we have to look towards new markets in the world. Inefficient and malfunctioning of industrial units in the public sector and the disinvestment policy introduced recently may not be able to turn these into productive profitable units because of lack of work culture and competition from the well established private units. The infrastructural facilities like power, water and means of communication and transportation etc., are hardly adequate to meet the expanding industrialization, urbanization, trade and commerce and other service sectors of economy.

Notwithstanding the grim reality on the industrial front, the agriculture scene is also not that rosy. In the recent past, there has not been any breakthrough in seed technology of the existing crops. Over the years, there has been increasing soil degradation, depletion of ground water level, pest menance, etc. Even the floods and drought conditions have not been adequately handled. Low priority to agricultural research and extension methods, patent laws for new varieties of plants and the methods of producing them under WTO and GATT agreements, farmers commiting suicides in some states due to failure of crops and indebtedness, are some of the new issues that need to be examined for agricultural development of the country.

Despite credit facilities provided to farmers through cooperative societies, and rural banking networks, most of the farmers are in the debt-trap of the non-institutional persons such as moneylenders and 'Aarthias' in the 'Mandis'. Due to the limited expansion of irrigation facilities there is a need to promote dry farming in certain parts of the country. Hill, forest and coastal areas need to produce the type of foods suitable to the cultural tastes of the people of these regions.

In a few years time, in certain regions of the country, there may be saturation point achieved in terms of the agricultural output. As such, there is an urgent need to bring agro-based industry as close and as early to the rural areas so that employment could be provided to the unemployed youth at the village level. That will also check migration of youth from rural areas to urban centres and prevent overcrowding of cities. In short, the thrust of India's economy has to be in the rural sector.

Due to pressure of population on land, agriculture may have limited prospect for generating employment in the rural areas. As such, allied agricultural industries, animal husbandry, pissiculture, fishery and revival of handicrafts to boost ethnic industries, may become necessary for employment generation especially among the educated youth. Infrastructural development in rural areas should further absorb labour force during the lean period of agriculture. Agricultural development should not be treated synonymous with rural development and in the 50th year of our independence, we should come forward with a National Policy on Rural Development. Three target groups namely the landless labourers, women and youth (both boys and girls in the age group of 14 to 24 years) need special attention for employment generation to raise their productivity and income levels.

Over the years, in India's economy, the tertiary sector has expanded much more than the primary and secondary sectors. There have been not much shift of labour force from agricultural to industrial sector of the economy while the expansion of the private sector has overburdened the public spending enormously. Domestic savings and even foreign savings for domestic investments are inadequate enough for development purposes and the economy based on international borrowings is bound to falter and instead of reducing the social and economic inequalities in between different social groups and regions, this may increase disparities. Economic development should not be left to the unintended consequences of market economic forces and efforts should be to involve people in productive economic pursuits through a dialogical and participatory approach.

The most striking question is whether the State apparatus or the polity can capture all the internalities and externalities of India's economy or not. The Indian National Congress, which got freedom for the country, being the single largest party, ruled the nation for nearly 45 years through the parliamentary democracy based on a Constitution advocating equality, social justice and fraternity. These equalitarian political goals were pursued through Five-Year Development Plans. Unfortunately, these resulted in lopsided development and instead of equality, we got increased inequality in our country. But, the parliamentary democracy struck roots and its fundamentals showed signs of maturity as despite changes in political parties and leadership structures, it gave some hope to have civil liberties and freedom. Of late, some thinking is being done to replace it with the presidential form of democracy. However, the merits and demerits of both the systems need to be examined.

The State apparatus, as a consequence of population rise, has expanded enormously. New States have been carved out with in the Union of India, and many new districts have been formed. Notwithstanding these changes, new political parties have merged in different states, since the central parties and leadership in power at different points of time failed to match with the needs and aspiration of people. This gave rise to capturing of power in different states by regional parties who showed cultural deftness in identifying themselves with the needs of the people. This also affected the power structure at the centre through parliamentary democracy. As a result, no single party could form a government at the centre and a culture of coalition government led by either one party or the other emerged. In fact, over the last fifty years, the centripetal forces got weakened and gave rise to centrifugal forces. These forces got strengthened partly due to certain provisions of reservation for Scheduled Castes, Scheduled Tribes, Backward Classes and certain other special categories in education, employment and election.

The Janata Dal coalition government at the centre led by V.P. Singh, despite stiff opposition from the protogonists of upper castes, went ahead with the implementation of the recommendations of Mandal Commissions with a proviso for further concessions to other backward classes identified by it. Due to limitation of the total reservations not to exceed 50 per cent of our population, the concept of creamy layer among these categories was evolved to help the weaker families enjoy the benefits of reservation adequately.

With better awareness among the reserved categories of population, they started asserting and making demand on the polity. The State was committed, as per Constitution, to provide them equality and social justice. They had faced oppression at the hand of not more 10 per cent of the upper castes in our society. Their protest movements bore results in terms of emergence of new political parties and leadership structures, safeguarding their interests vis-a-vis others. This resulted into mushrooming of political parties at the regional level in each state which besides taking care of the reserved categories also vouched for the minority communities in their respective states. However, this led to serious political consequences and gave rise to divisive forces promoting casteism and communalism in our society. Worse than that, the political differentiation processes over the last five decades, have thrown up configurations and combinations that have promoted commercialization and criminalization of politics. This has a destabilizing aspect in our society and our moral social order is observed to be at the lowest ebb.

Political arithmetic based on ethnic, linguistic, religious, caste and class lines, political alliances of convenience rather than on ideological or issue base, and political coalitions to capture power in the state assembly or parliament are the tactics or strategies common with the politicians. Acrimony, fist fights, shouting, behaviour below the acceptable decency level by the elected representatives of people in the state legislatures and parliament, send shockwaves to the elites and the masses alike and one starts doubting they future of democracy in our country.

Any society is basically a moral society and what is right or wrong has to be determined by the people at the helm of affairs. These people have to set the example of probity by showing accountability of their acts and transparency in their dealings. Politicians apart, in the state apparatus, we have now an enlarged bureaucracy entrusted with the task of planning and implementing the development issues of the people. The hierarchical arrangement within the bureaucracy, centralized command, rigid rules and regulations and anti-development attitude among bureaucrats at different levels has created situations of corruption, nepotism and favouritism. These bureaucrats because of mercenary tendencies due to materialistic values have got inleague with most of the politicians and together they pose threat to the moral order of our society. These are dangerous trends and provide encouragement to a corrupt society based on selfish motives.

In the above backdrop, the state or the polity can neither capture the internalities and the externalities of the economy nor could it provide a lead towards a civil society. A host of scandals, affairs and crises have appeared on the national scene. These have affected the legal codes and generated a Constitutional crisis for a nation. Further, the linguistic ethnocentrism has weakened the process of having universalistic ties in between our people so necessary for a civil society. The development process, though raised hopes and aspirations of people, yet the plans failed to relate the activities to the expected cultural code of a large majority. This gave rise to frustration on the part of many and we witnessed a bouts or riots, bomb explosions, violence and strikes creating more chaos than order in the society due to aggressive or regressive behaviour of these persons.

Due to vested interests, the power elites have not functioned in pluralized way and that has led to the leadership crisis in the country. Further, they do not want to vacate their power positions for others and that has bred corruption of the worst order in the system. A democratic system, it is argued, is bound to generate strifes, tensions and disruptions within a social system. However, these need to be managed to reduce them to the minimum. However, it is observed that the ideals of civil society and the mechanisms to accomplish these have played feebly and inadequately in our society. If these tensions are not contained within reasonable limits, it will lead to an anarchic state in our country (Mehta, 1997b).

Can, we, as a nation afford such a situation? The system, constituting the economy and the state or the polity, needs to be shaken vigorously to reorganize itself in such a manner as to deliver the goods to the people and accomplish the goals of a good society based on equality, social justice and probity. If the leadership crisis is to be averted in our society, then the leadership structures should be sensitive to the cultural needs of the people, rather than exploiting cultural symbols like 'Mandal', 'Mandir' and 'Masjid' to woo the voters for maintaining their power positions. Even the economic activities to be pursued should be in relevance with the needs of the people, only then a perfect "uncoupling" of the economy and the state can be accomplished.

Do the politico-economic forces affect the socio-cultural changes or the reverse of that is true? This has been debated enough and all set of factors, economic, political, social and cultural are interrelated within a societal system to provide a social order. Anyway, all economic phenomena are social in nature and together, these constitute the total reality. As such, in terms of social, structural and organizational arrangements in our society, rigid hierarchical relationships stratify us on caste, class, age, sex and ethanic bases. The institution of caste is cardinal to the understanding of Indian society. The concept of "purity-pollution" based on rituals of the Hindus (more than 80 per cent of our population is that of Hindus and in the social analysis of our society, the Hindu modal values prevail).

Since caste and class inheres with each other in our setting, the land and the industrial-cum-commercial relationships are determined by these dimensions. There is exploitation, oppression and discrimination of people belonging to lower castes and classes (invariably these are highly correlated in our setting) by the upper castes and classes. Peasant movements with the support of certain ideological parties (CPI(M) and CPI) waged caste wars in a state like Bihar in between the upper and lower castes. Labour movements in the industrial and agricultural sectors, have benefitted labourers marginally, though the major benefits have been taken away by the upper caste and class owners and managers. Women and human right activists have launched new movements to get justice for the weaker sections of the society, including women. Reservation policy in education, employment and election for SCs, STs, BCs and OBCs, has helped many go-getters among them to have social mobility and make improvements in their respective positions. Besides, NGOs have taken up a number of development initiatives in different sectors of economy in various parts of the country to make people aware and ensure their participation in economic activities for a better life.

Expansion of education, trade and commerce, industrialization, green and white revolution in certain parts of the country, technological breakthroughs, occupational diversification, political consciousness and social movements, have contributed significantly in increasing the middle class in our society. Despite that the caste and kinship solidarities are still intact to a large extent. Although the sharing of food in between different caste groups is no longer a taboo, yet the marriages are generally contracted within a caste group. Further, besides the onset of the process of nuclearization of families, family and kinship networks are strong and people in need of help, always look towards them. In this respect, one can pose a question whether the modernising roles of individuals as advocated by changes in values of individuals by the "Modernization" paradigm can lead to breaking up the caste and kinship solidarities in our society. Industrialising and the urbanising influences may play a positive role in that direction. But we need to preserve our family structure as this is the strength of our society. Instead of promoting individual entrepreneurship, there is a need to provide family enterprise. This may help us in maintaining social solidarity of our society through intensive and extensive kinship networks. However, this may not help us in liquidating the caste solidarity which may become a hindrance to the development of our society.

Over the years, the modernising influence in our country has been so strong that they have brought in new values and our society is tending to become materialistic. This has affected our social relationship as well because now in our relationships with others, we are guided by mercenary rather than altruistic values. Self-orientation has become dominant and our concern for others and helping the needy persons appear to have been overshadowed by the material consideration. There is a need to evaluate the new values along with the old ones prevalent in religious scriptures. In assessing our social reality, one must be guided by the fact that in urban India, especially in the metropolitan cities, there is an increasing domination of modern westernized values over the traditional Indian values, whereas in the rural India, there is still a greater adherance to the traditional values, though a penetration of modern values is also visible to a large extent.

Another reality that has emerged on the scene is that the democratic values and forces through parliamentary democracy during the last five decades have, instead of equalising people in different caste groups, highly politicized them and the factor of caste is reckoned with in Indian politics. Caste has assumed greater significance in political relationships and our social structural and organizational arrangements have been influenced by this very factor. Casteism in politics has promoted corruption, favouratism and nepotism at all levels and caste instead of being an integrative mechanism in our society, is functioning as a divisive force.

Strong ethnic identities based on caste, kinship ties, language and territory, as a part of our culture, are being exploited for corrupting the economy and the state or the polity. This has serious implications for the "lifeworld" constituting the public and the private spheres. The public, that is the consumers, are at large the beneficiaries of the economic pursuits launched by the state, but it is affected adversely in acquiring values that are conducive to equality, social justice and probity; instead, they are lured by values of profit motive, self-orientation, material gains and individualism. These provide conflicting value situations in a democratic set-up and need to be resolved through education of public so that a greater commitment to development could be exhibited in the 'private' sphere representing the labour force.

Another social reality of the Indian society is that it is multi-religious and linguistic in character. This brings in the element of diversity within a unified whole. Despite so many religious adherances, the dominant among them being Hinduism, Islam, Christianity, Buddhism, Sikhism and Jainism, people do share many ways of life and cultural traits which bind them together as Indians. Thus, they do represent a composite culture woven of different yarn and colours. Democracy brought in the concept of secularism into the life of people belonging to different religions. Secularism either understood as 'above' religions or tolerance of one religion group towards the other is a modern value. This is propogated as a part of "Modernization" paradigm which advocates homogenization of various groups into one universal civilization.

The western civilization is being considered as an evolved form of civilization by the developed world. Because of the superiority of technology and the attainment of the value of freedom, it is suggested that we are all moving towards a "universal civilization" through cultural togetherness of humanity and the increasing acceptance of common values, beliefs and institutions. According to Huntington, the central elements of any civilization are language and religion. If at all, there is an emergence of a universal civilization due to end of cold war because the only alternative to communism now is liberal democracy and people would rush to embrace the western liberalism, then it is not understood as to why there are more fundamental divisions of ethnicity, religions and civilizations that are generating conflicts of new kinds. In this context, it is argued that people define themselves by what makes them different from others in a particular context. The things that mean most to them are ancestry, religion, language, history, values, customs and institutions. In short, people identify with cultural groups such as tribes, ethnic groups, religious communities, nations and at the broadest level, civilizations. As such, it is suggested that the western leaders, instead of intervening in the affairs of other civilizations, should preserve and renew qualities of its own civilization. Any attempt to suggest universal civilization to other civilizations may be dangerous and may lead to instability in the world (Huntington, 1998). Even in the dimensions of language, modernization failed to provide homogenization of western nations, as in Europe alone, there are more than 3000 languages spoken.

In the context of our society, Hindus constitute an ancient civilization and Hinduism has existed on our subcontinent since at least 1500 B.C. in one form or the other. This is stated to be central to the culture of India since the second millennium B.C. Islam, which originated in Arabian peninsula in the seventh century A.D., spread across various regions and eastward into central Asia, the Indian subcontinent. Modern India represents a mix of Hindu and Islamic civilizations (Huntington, 1998).

In the above context, development of people in our sub-continent has to be in congruence with the core values upheld by our population. Religion should serve the humanity instead of enslaving mankind. It is often said that faith begins when science fails. Development of our people has to be based on scientific religious ideology. Our elites, by that ideology, shall have to bid farewell to the monolithic pyramidal structurarization of religion and evolve a new religion of development based on values fostering human progress. If "Protestant ethic" of Calvinism could be a moving spirit to the rise of capitalism in Europe, there is no doubt about the effectiveness of theory of action (Karma) advocated by Lord Krishna in the Holy Bhagwat Gita, as an inspiring motive for people to work for the betterment of mankind. We shall have to infuse certain values of probity, frugality, need rather greed, humanitarianism, tolerance and fraternity among us and keep the materialistic values at the minimum level in our day-to-day life.

While constructing the Indian social reality, I have indulged into the nature of development initiatives that may go along with our economy, polity, social arrangements of relationships, religious adherences and values. The demographic factor of population rise and density cuts across all these dimensions and make deep inroads into the development initiatives for a good society. However, these elements of our societal structure will have to operate within our geo-physical setting. Based on this analysis, which is not exhaustic, an attempt will be made to visualize development of our people in a sociological perspective.

Development: A Sociological Perspective

Development has remained the domain of the economists while the sociologists have always been treated marginally.

However, of late, it is recognized that without consideration of the socio-cultural and political configurations, development is a herculean task in the context of developing nations. A paradigm shift in development in our setting from a socialistic pattern of society to a market economy has brought in more contradictions in the development planning. It is argued in certain quarters that if the liberal market economic forces are to determine the courses of development in our country, then what is the need of planned development efforts? Over the last one decade or so, there have been tremendous changes in our society at a much faster pace than before. This has brought about the political mobilization of masses (especially the Dalits, Women and Peasants) and ushered in certain amount of social mobility among some segments of our population. We had an enlarged middle class which provided a market with an increased number of consumers for durable and undurable goods.

But at the same time, due to population rise, the number of illiterate and malnourished poor in absolute term increased. The entry of multinationals into our economy in the last decade or so has overshadowed the local entrepreneurs and many of the smaller and sick units have been eaten up by the big and giant companies. This has given rise to new tastes and preferences among the people, especially in the metropolitan cities in the country, and the lifestyle of urban elites and middle and upper rich classes has started matching the lifestyle of western nations. Some of the consumer goods have also penetrated into the rural areas and here too certain segments of the population are being influenced by western cultural patterns. However, the rural and urban poverty, cannot be left to the vagaries of market economic forces, and one has to make planned development efforts to alleviate them from the life of drudgery.

As sociologists, we are interested with the conditions in which people live. We have to analyse the conditions of existence of poverty, anticipate consequences and provide policy leads for suitable interventions. This brings in into focus the need of a sociological perspective on development.

What is a sociological perspective on development? Purists among the sociologists may speak of a theory of social change but to my thinking, there is no single theory coherent in nature that explains the phenomena of social change and development. As sociologists, we are interested in studying societies with a view to understand the patterns of action and interaction among people embodying norms, values, standards and sanctions for a social order aimed at progress and prosperity of its people.

As such, the first prerequisite for a sociological perspective on development is to place "people" in the centre stage. People to people communication is cardinal in energising and empowering them to take appropriate decisions on the problems faced by them and make them active social actors to tackle these. Development should not only rely on econocentric or technocentric models but be guided by people, their institutions, their knowledge, their forms of social organization to develop themselves for attaining the goal of a good society without tensions, strifes and disruptions.

Secondly, the thrust of a sociological perspective has to be on social relations. Social relations are important in human development. An analysis of 51 poor countries showed that those countries whose citizens enjoyed greater political and civil liberties also experienced large improvements in life expectancy at birth, real income per head and infant survival rates (Das Gupta and Weale, 1992).

These hard indicators of development apart, we have to evolve some descriptive-cum-analytical indicators to show improvement in landlord-labour, employer-employee and industrial owner-manager-worker relationships, in favour of the latter. In other words, development initiatives should be such as to induce alternatives in social structural relationships. With these changes in sociol arrangements constituting various institutional apparatuses, there is some possibility of inducing development to the exploited persons in the interactional framework.

This will call for a social analysis of our society based on an analytical description coherent enough to be predictive and prescriptive. There are "contemporary variations among existing cultures" (Mead, 1976) and to capture these, the Sociology and Anthropology must combine their bodies of knowledge and methods. Analysis of social relations through multidisciplinary methods, should also throw light on economic, political and cultural ties to provide a complete understanding of the social fabric of the society for deciding upon the path of collective action for the development of the people.

Thirdly, a sociological perspective on development should emphasize on "new" social movements within a society. Social movements are significant for transforming the society through their leadership and character of ideology. "New" social movements through their agents and agencies can enthuse and imbibe new values (appetitive or normative in types; cognitive, affective and connotive in components and having different levels of abstraction in the descending order: value, value orientation, attitude and opinion) among the people and this shift in their value system may result in the formation of a new culture conductive to the development of those who need most attention. Value change in a society can bring about through a change in information or through political, economic and technological change. Further, for value change, the levels of analysis (individuals, groups, institutions and society) and area of change (social conditions, experiences and attitudes towards these conditions, goals, norms and standards) are to be taken into account (Rosenberg, 1981).

"New" social movements (youth, women, peasants, human right activists, activists in child labour, health hazards such as AIDS, smoking, drug addiction, etc., population control, adult literacy campaigns, labour and workers' welfare, etc.) often do not succeed in accomplishing their set goals mainly because of opposition from the established institutional apparatus of the state and non-conformity to the established norms and rules of the polity and the economy. However, they set in motion a chain reaction of activities which vibrate the masses through a public awarness process and mobilize them to make demands on the establishment for a desired change. These "new" social movements, through mobilization process of the masses, enlarge the public sphere, a constituent of the "lifeworld" and bring into fold an increased number of persons in the consumer net for new economic tastes suitable to the needs of the people.

In mobilizing people, another aspect of sociological perspective in development is to initiate the process of decentralization for an active participation of people in the developmental activities. Instead of the economy and the state entering the life sustaining and welfare activities of people, people themselves should become the masters of their own destiny. They should find social spaces in the societal structure and get out of the confines of the politico-economic set-up. Nearly half of the population in this country is women. Besides, youth (boys and girls in the age group of 14-24 years) constitute a substantial population and nearly one-third people in villages are landless labourers. All these social groups and many more valuables to the participatory model of development can be mobilized to develop themselves and their families through economic pursuits that suit their cultural environments.

Participation of people in development activities can generate greater commitment in them for their sustained growth. There is a need to make people's organizations more organized internally so that they become better aware of their power and that would enhance their mobilization capacity. People can start on their own, some of the small production oriented projects, production support service projects and social service projects with the help of NGOs, the committed social activists, intellectuals and social workers. These small scale-efforts in different locations and regions can stimulate changes in economic and social spheres and the participation of people in the development activities will enhance the commitment of the "private" sphere, that is the labour force, as a constituent of the "lifeworld".

In the context of the developing nation, the next aspect of sociological perspective on development, should be a thrust on human resource development. The most important characteristic of the poor that needs a change for reviewing poverty, and reducing social and economic inequalities in the developing nations is education, not only in formal sense but also in terms of skills. Primary education is an important means for raising productivity and hence growth. This holds good for improvement in health and nutrition of the people as well (Mehta, 1997b). Data estimation for 88 developing countries by Wheeler (1980) and Morris (1982) indicate a significant impact on growth rates from increase in caloric intake and literacy rates. Morris's study found that primary education enrollments showed favourable effects on growth rates of per capita income.

In our case, besides expansion of health care and education, population control especially among the poor will help them to overcome their poor conditions of living. Education is critical not only for making parliamentary democracy a success by providing people, the equality and the social justice but it is essential also for the advancement of science and technology and so, crucial for advancement of the developing societies. Population rise has been a destabilizing factor for development and we need to have a quality of population so that people become knowledgeable and skilful to be more productive for economic pursuits. The socio-political, economic and cultural settings warrant a new health system based on decentralized planning for a participative process through the involvement and commitment of community leaders to be evolved for our society which is consistent with our needs and resources (Mehta, 1992).

Human development is a necessary as well as an essential prerequisite for societal development and the social service oriented changes such as education, health care and population control, can go a long-way in affecting the development processes and transforming the society for a new social order. In short, a sociological perspective on development would need placing people in the centre stage of development, involving people in development, deconcentration of power and decentralization of people in developmental activities, sensitizing the masses through personal and impersonal channels of communication, education and health care for raising productivity, technological innovations for conservation and renewal of energy and natural resources, empowerment of women, supporting moral along with material values, developing the skill of the poor to raise their purchasing power and curbing the population of the developing nations (Mehta, 1997).

The econocentric and technocentric models of development need to take the sociological perspective into account as without this the development of developing nations including India, can cause greater contradictions within the social system and that may consequently promote maldevelopment and our society may have to face a developmental crisis. As such, development in the context of developing nations has to be people's focused, people's directed and people's involved. This is what a sociological perspective on development should be.

References

Brand, A., (1990), *The Fore of Reason: An Introduction to Habermas's 'Theory of Communication Action*, London, Allen and Unwin.

Cernea, Michael, M., (1996), *Social Organization and Development Anthropology*: The 1995 Malinowski Award Lecture, Washington D. C., The World Bank.

Crook, S., et al. (1992), *Postmodernization: Changes in Advanced Society*, London, Sage.

Das Gupta, Partha and Martin Weale, (1992), "On Measuring the Quality of Life", *World Development*, Vol. 20, No. 1 (January).

Gill, S.S., (1998), "Issue of Rural Development: Budgetary Rhetoric and Reality", Chandigarh, *The Tribune*, June 10.

Haan, Jacob de and Siermann, L.J., (1996), "Political Instability, Freedom and Economic Growth: Some Further Evidence", *Economic Development and Cultural Change*, Vol. 44, No. 2 (January).

Habermas, J., (1984), *Theory of Communicative Action*, Vol. I, Reason and the Rationalization of Society, London, Heinemann.

Habermas, J., (1987), *Theory of Communicative Action*, Vol. 2, *Lifeworld and System: A Critique of Functionalist Reason*, Cambridge, Polity Press.

Haubert Maxime, (1991), "The Sociology of Development: What Sociology? What Development", *The European Journal of Development Research*, Vol. 3, No. 2 (December).

Huntnigton, P. Samuel, (1998), "Clash of Civilization: The Many Faces of the Future", New Delhi, *SPAN*, Vol. XXXIX, No. 3 (May, June), pp. 18-21.

Malinowski, Bronislaw, (1961), *The Dynamics of Cultural Change*, New Haven, Connecticut.

Mead, Margaret, (1976), "Applied Anthropology: The State of the Art", in Anthony F.C. Wollace and Assoc., (eds.). *Perspectives on Anthropology*, Washington, D.C. American Anthropological Association.

Mehta, S. R., (1992), *Society and Health: A Sociological Perspective*, New Delhi, Vikas Publishing House Pvt. Ltd.

Mehta, S. R., (1997) (ed.), *Poverty, Population and Sustainable Development*, Jaipur, Rawat Publications.

Mehta, S. R. (1997b), "Backwardness and Civil Society" in Mehta, S. R. (ed.), *Poverty Population and Sustainable Development*. Jaipur, Rawat Publications, pp. 84-104.

Mink, Stephan, D., (1993), *Poverty, Population and the Environment*, Washington, D. C., The World Bank, Discussion paper.

Moorris, Robin, (1982), Economic Growth in Cross Section" (Mimeo). Washington, D.C., The World Bank as quoted in Cardoso, E. and A. Helwege (1992). "Below the Line, Poverty in Latin America", *World Development*, Vol. 20, No. 1 (January).

Rosenberg, Karl Erik, (1981), "Mass Media and Social Change: Some Current Approaches" in Katz E. and Tamas Szecsko (eds), *Mass Media and Social Change*, London, Sage Publications.

Seambler, Graham, (1996), "The 'Project of Modernity' and Parameters in critical sociology". *Sociology*, The Journal of the British Sociological Association, Vol. 30, No. 3, (August), pp. 567-81.

Wheeler, David, (1980), "Human Resource Development and Economic Growth in Developing Countries: A Simulation Model", World Bank Staff Working Paper as quoted in Cordoso and Helwege, *op. cit.*

Index